THIS BOOK BELONGS TO THE LIBRARY OF

Published by Brave Hill Publishing

www.wonderfulwanderingwagon.com

Cover and Internal Illustrations by Aslan Dominique

First Edition

HARDBACK ISBN 978-1-959158-00-4

PAPERBACK ISBN 978-1-959158-01-1

EBOOK ISBN 978-1-959158-02-8

This is a work of fiction, and while many characters are inspired by real people and animals all events are entirely made up.
Honor the cat does not take on business consulting clients and is not interested in any business investing, she mostly naps and models for our Instagram page @wonderfulwanderingwagon.

THE WONDERFUL WANDERING WAGON

by

JOE AND JEN ROBERSON
Illustrated by Aslan Dominique

BRAVE HILL
PUBLISHING

DEDICATED TO:

the Roberson children
May the Lord keep you as you grow
and learn how to use your skills
for His glory to grow His Kingdom.

CONTENTS

PROLOGUE 2
CHAPTER I 8
CHAPTER II 16
CHAPTER III 24
CHAPTER IV 30
CHAPTER V 36
CHAPTER VI 42
CHAPTER VII 48
CHAPTER VIII 56
CHAPTER IX 66
CHAPTER X 72
CHAPTER XI 82
CHAPTER XII 92
CHAPTER XIII 98
CHAPTER XIV 108
CHAPTER XV 114
CHAPTER XVI 126
CHAPTER XVII 134
CHAPTER XVIII 140
CHAPTER XIX 146
CHAPTER XX 152
EPILOGUE 162

PROLOGUE

"No one is ever born at the wrong time or in the wrong place. Some of us just take a while to get where we need to be, while others of us get there whether we want to go or not. In the end, we all are born in the place we should be born in and end up where we should be going. The path is different for each of us. For some of us, it is more wonderful than others, but all of us have an important place to be at our exact moment."

—*Grandpa Bishop*

The fire crackled in the large stone hearth of the old house, filling the room with heat and comfort. Two couples sat silently in their rocking chairs as they drank their tea from wooden mugs, caught up in thoughts about what was to come. Outside, the autumn air had picked up the crispness of the first freeze, and the lengthening nights created more opportunities for cozy fireside conversations. The wind wisped through the shakes and pushed in under the large oaken door. The leaves had changed colors a few weeks before, and exactly as the elves had predicted in the almanac, this year, it appeared that winter cold would arrive earlier than normal. In front of the hearth on the wooden floor was a grand fur rug, and in the middle of the rug was a large curled-up cat.

"She might leave this year, might be the next," the oldest man said, pointing at the cat. "I doubt it'll be longer than that since Sinclair is about to turn fifteen."

"Is there any way to talk her out of it?" asked the younger of the two women. "I'm just not sure that he's ready to be by himself."

The younger man smiled to himself and gently took his wife's hand. "Mary, you know that this is part of what happens in our family. Trying to get Honor to change her mind about something is never easy, let alone when it's as important as this. Sinclair will be fine."

The older lady smiled and, with a happy lilt, added her bit. "I wasn't ready when Charles went out, either, Mary, but every child has to grow up at some point. You two have done a great job preparing him, and we can't watch over them for their whole lives. He may not know what's coming, but he's been given a good base to know how to run his own store."

"I know, Anabelle. It's just that I'm still not sure he's ready to be by himself. Charles didn't have any siblings, so he had to keep up with the adults, but Sinclair has been with his brother and sisters his whole life. He's not nearly as competent as I remember Charles being. Charles just knew how to do everything."

At that statement, the cat looked up from her nap and gave Mary a curious stare. Charles, the younger of the men, started to laugh. “Sweetheart, I think if Honor could talk to you, she would be happy to tell you of my utter incompetence when I was first starting out. I didn’t know what I was doing, but no one really does when they start out. It’s just part of the journey, and that’s something that I learned with Honor. I will say, though—if I could have taken my best friend, Edward, when I left, I would have. It sure would have been nice to have someone to talk through problems with when things got sticky. Was there someone you would have taken, Dad?”

“Yes, I would have taken your uncle Chuck. If Great-Great-Grandpa Alexander’s business dealings hadn’t included a nondisclosure agreement with Honor’s sire, we would have been able to tell your uncle, and I would have been able to find him when I finished my first trip. As it was, before I finished my first cycle, your grandpa had passed away and Charles had signed up as a caravan guard. I was never able to find him again. That will not happen to Sinclair.”

“It will be hard on his siblings for him to disappear, but we can be there for the other kids, and they won’t worry as much if we don’t worry ourselves,” Charles said before sipping on his mug.

“I just wish he had someone who could go with him and help him out,” Mary said, looking at the fire and then the cat.

Honor stood up slowly and stretched. She was the most gorgeous cat, with long smoky fur and an angular face that gave her a touch of wildness despite her friendly personality. Her ears had cute tufts growing out of them, and her long hair fell around her head like a mane. As a fully grown Maine coon, she was noticeably larger than your typical house cat, but instead of making her imposing, her size just made her easier to snuggle. Honor chirped a little, walked over to Mary, and climbed up into her lap. She rubbed her head under Mary's chin then settled down, taking up her full lap, and started to purr.

Anabelle giggled and gave a bright smile. "See, Mary—I think Honor is telling you not to worry. Besides, it might not even be this year. Charles was sixteen before he went."

"I still think—"

That was all Mary got out of her mouth before Honor meowed loudly and bumped her mug, spilling the hot tea on the blanket. Honor primly jumped off her lap as Mary yelped and the others scrambled to grab a towel.

"Honor, that wasn't necessary! I know you have been good to our family and have always taken care of the boys when you took them out. I just worry about my baby boy being alone. He's never been by himself like that before," Mary moaned as she dried herself off.

Honor chirped and moved to the hearth. She slowly stretched her body and settled down into a couchant pose, with her tail wrapped slightly around her body and twitching back and forth at the tip like a feather duster. She looked as regal as any animal could. A slight smirk played across her face as though she knew more than anyone around her.

Alexander looked at the other three as they sat back down. "I guess we should see if we can get Sinclair a good pack to start with. If I could, I would send him with a wagonload of goods and a full library to help him plan. It could be any day now, so tomorrow, we should head to town and get a bag ready to make the first few days easier on him."

"We can leave the other children here so that he won't be alone," said Mary. "That way, we can get back with the bag and tell him to never leave the house without it."

CHAPTER ONE

"We order our calendar based on the loss of the third moon, Daisy, for at that time, the three sisters became two, and everything changed. Our nights got darker, our tides got bigger, the kingdom collapsed, and all the races got lifebooks with their classes and quests."

—*A History of the Purvas: Jonathan Counting - Two Sisters 1049*

Sinclair woke up in the guest loft of one of his grandpa's barns. The sun was just starting to peek through the loft door, and a gray, fluffy weight sat presumptuously on his chest as he attempted unsuccessfully to sit up. He slowly opened his eyes and saw Honor glaring down at him as if to say, *Are you getting up anytime soon?*

"All right, Honor, I'm getting up," Sinclair said as he got out from under the blankets.

The air was cold, but at least he didn't have to share a room anymore. He was almost fifteen, and this was the first year that he could sleep in the hayloft by himself, so he really didn't mind the chill if it meant he didn't have to hear his brother blabber on at night. Also, Honor seemed to prefer the barn loft, although Sinclair wasn't quite sure how she got in, considering cats didn't typically climb ladders.

Sinclair brushed the hay off himself, went over to the loft door, and opened it the rest of the way. A blast of cold air hit him in the face as the sun rose over the trees, its rays lighting up the morning fog that lay across the pastures near his grandpa's homestead. Invigorated by the chill, Sinclair grabbed the rope pulley that hung from the hay hood and stepped out of the second-floor door. Holding on with one arm, he dangled, taking a brief look at the world before he triggered the handle and fell, laughing all the way to the ground.

Sinclair stood up, smiling and laughing. He raised his fists victoriously into the air and yelled, "I love doing that!"

As he crossed the field, the smell of bacon cooking on a fire greeted his nose. His stomach rumbled, so he ran the last fifty feet to his grandpa's large stone house. A few wood shakes needed to be fixed, which meant that he was likely going to be up on the roof later in the week with his dad.

When he walked through the door, the rest of the family was already awake and sitting at the table. Sinclair quickly realized that his three siblings were most of the way done with their food and were not going to let his lateness pass unannounced.

"Look who decided to wake up," the oldest girl said. Although Penelope was a year younger than Sinclair, she clearly didn't see that as a reason to keep her thoughts to herself. Besides, this was one of the three weeks that they were both fourteen, and she was not going to miss an opportunity to comment on her brother's behavior.

"Awww, Pen," Gretchen said. "You *sh*ould be ni*c*e to him. He had to walk all the way from *th*e barn, and besides, tomo*rr*ow's his bir*th*day."

"Thank you, Gretchen," Sinclair said. "I always knew you were the nice one."

Gretchen beamed. She might have trouble being understood sometimes, but if there was anything the twelve-year-old knew how to do, it was get on someone's good side.

Sinclair breathed a sigh of relief as he sat down at the table. Life was good. Tomorrow, he would be offered the opportunity to choose his class, which would give him new skills and set him up for a lifetime of adventure and excitement. Adventure and excitement *without* his siblings. He couldn't wait. It wasn't that he didn't love his siblings, but they were always causing issues for him and holding him back. It would be so much easier without them around to make him mad.

As Sinclair looked off into space, dreaming about the adventures that lay ahead, a slight movement caught his eye. Almost on cue, his eight-year-old brother was reaching toward the bacon on Sinclair's plate, a mischievous smile on his face.

"Hey, that's my bacon!" Sinclair grabbed Warren's hand.

"Dad! Sinclair hurt me!" Warren whined.

"He was stealing my bacon!" Sinclair argued.

"Was not! Just acted like it, but if you'd been here to start with, I wouldn't have had the chance."

"Boys! Behave," Charles Bishop commanded. "Sinclair, you shouldn't have hurt your brother over bacon. Warren, it's not nice to steal your brother's bacon right in front of him."

"So if I stole it before he came in, it would be okay?" Warren asked.

"Well, now that you ask that, no." Their father smiled. "Warren, you need to apologize to your brother for trying to take his bacon, and, Sinclair, you need to apologize for hurting your brother.

"I'm sorry, Warren," Sinclair muttered.

"I know you are, but do you apologize?" Warren quipped with an ear-to-ear grin and his eyes wider than wide.

Sinclair clenched his fist as he looked at his brother's smug little face. He could feel the anger welling up in his chest as he considered how fun it would be to wipe the smile away with his chair. His thoughts were quickly interrupted by Charles clearing his throat.

"Warren, please forgive me for hurting you for trying to steal my bacon," Sinclair mumbled.

"I might forgive you once my hand stops hurting," Warren said.

"Dad! Warren won't forgive me when I ask."

"Sinclair, you can't control the actions of others, only your own." Their dad took another bite of a muffin. "When we genuinely ask someone to forgive us and take steps to make it right, we have done our part as best we can. It's up to them if they're going to forgive. Owning our mistakes is part of growing up, and being quick to ask for forgiveness and quick to forgive is also part of it. That said, Warren, if you cultivate a habit of withholding forgiveness, then you only hurt yourself. You break the relationship that you have with your brother, and you never know when that might matter."

Warren looked at his brother and then looked down. Charles's words must have spoken truth to his heart, because something shifted in the boy. "Sinclair, I'm really sorry for going after your bacon. Will you forgive me?"

Sinclair saw the shift in his brother and felt bad. He really had overreacted, and he could see his brother was truly sorry. "I guess I would have done the same if you hadn't been here. I do forgive you. I'm sorry I wasn't more self-controlled and allowed my anger to rule me. Is your hand okay?"

Sinclair turned his head back from his brother as he heard Gretchen giggle. Then he saw that his bacon was gone from his plate, and Honor was scampering off the table with the strip of meat in her mouth.

“Honor! You too?” cried the teenager.

From the kitchen hearth, Grandma Bishop said, “Sinclair, there’s plenty more bacon over here for you. Come get some, and make sure you guard it. Honor loves the stuff.”

CHAPTER TWO

"Choosing your class is what makes a child an adult—at least, it has for the past thousand years or so. Make sure you pick something good, because it can help you grow in ways you can't imagine."

—Count Dramouth III - Two Sisters 1149

"So, Sinclair, tomorrow's your birthday. Have you figured out what class you are going to pick?" Penelope asked.

"Well, I thought that it might be nice to get out and see the world. I know Mom and Dad have been training us to take over the store, but I was hoping I might do that after I spent some time adventuring. I thought I might pick up an adventurer's class and get involved with the local Adventurers Guild. Plus, we live near a dungeon." Sinclair gave her a big smile.

"Yeah, you would make a great berserker—you have the temper of one. The only thing is, you have the body of a store clerk, so that might not work," Warren stated.

Warren was famous for his honest "observations." While many might be offended by his truthfulness, he generally didn't mean anything negative by his statements. To him, they were simply matters of fact.

Sinclair took his brother's statements in stride and went down the logical route instead. "Ren, I wouldn't go for a berserker. I know I'm way too small. I was thinking I might be fast enough that I could be a fighter, or if I got lucky, I could be a sword dancer," he said, shoveling food in his mouth.

Their mom cleared her throat. "Now, Sinclair, I know that the adventurers that come into the shop seem amazing, but many of the young ones find that it's too hard, and then they have a class they can't use. Promise us that you will talk to us about your class first."

"*Mom*, I know it's hard and dangerous to go into the dungeon, but that doesn't have to be the only place I work. I could be a ranger and go around the woods, finding all sorts of things people would want to buy." Sinclair knew his argument didn't make much sense, but he was only trying to justify his decision. "It's not like there are any class skills that are super special for the store clerk," he said with a huff.

"Son, before you choose, talk with us. The class that you can choose when you turn fifteen is a huge part of becoming an adult. You can't pick another one until get your first class to level ten, you turn twenty-five, or you go to an academy. Also, there are rare and ultra-rare classes that we can see about getting triggered for you, based on what you have around." Charles Bishop smiled.

"I bet Grandpa has an adventure class!" Sinclair exclaimed with all the wonder of a grandchild.

Alexander Bishop laughed from his rocking chair near the fire and started to talk across the small, very packed room. "Well, I do, but it wasn't my first class. It was my second. I had found myself in quite a predicament, and it was a good thing the option showed up."

"What happened, Grandpa?" Warren moved in closer, and his eyes widened.

Alexander threw Charles a knowing glance and smiled. "It's kind of hard to talk about, but I'll see what I can do." He rubbed his hands together and leaned forward on his rocker.

Honor, who was by the fire, hopped up into Alexander's lap and then climbed onto his shoulder and started to purr. He reached up and scratched her head as she laid herself behind his neck, over both shoulders, and started to swat his face with her tail.

Alexander grinned and got his storytelling voice ready with a cough. "Well, let's see. I got my second class when I was nineteen, which is unique in and of itself. It's 1149 now, and I'm sixty, so that would have been in the year of Two Sisters 1108. I was in a town a long way off from here, working with my business partner, and I'd just made a really dumb mistake. I thought that I could make more money if I went right into the woods and gathered the alchemical ingredients myself instead of buying them from someone else.

"You see, the thing is, if you don't know what something looks like or where you are in the woods, it's really easy to get lost and grab the wrong thing. I was looking for the leaves of the red passion root, which I could sell at the next place I was going for a lot of money. I knew the plant grew around this town. However, so did everyone else, so it was pretty expensive to buy outright. I wanted to make a good bit of money, and I wanted to make it fast, because there was this nice lady I'd met a few weeks before who I wanted to get to know better.

Alexander smiled over at Grandma Bishop and winked. "I did end up getting to know her better, but this whole mess set me back a good two years with what I was trying to do. Anyways, I was out in the woods, lost as could be, with no idea what the leaves of the red passion root looked like if they weren't already dried for sale. As I was wandering around, I heard a crack and suddenly found myself falling into darkness as the stick I had just stepped on gave way."

"The next thing I knew, I was neck-deep in cold water as I realized I'd fallen into underground lake. As my eyes adjusted to the light, I found myself in a fairly large cave, and while I couldn't tell for sure, my guess is I was about twenty-five feet from the opening, which seemed to be right in the middle of a natural dome. All I had with me was my day pack. Unfortunately, I'd made the mistake of going out without a rope."

Grandpa said in a very firm voice and with a hidden grin, "Remember, kids, you will always want it if you hadn't got it! So, there I was in a cave, with no rope and no way up. Thankfully, I was able to climb out of the pool, and I want to say I'd spent about three days searching the branches of the cave, looking for an exit, when I came to a door. Now, let me be the first to tell you—if those adventurers your parents sell to haven't done it already—doors are not a natural part of a cave. If you are in a cave, and there's a door, then either someone put it there, or it's a dungeon door."

The kids gasped. The youngest three had moved close to their grandpa as he was telling his tale and sat on the fur rug, looking up at him and his fluffy cat necklace.

Alexander continued. "I didn't know it at the time, but the door in front of me was a new dungeon that had just formed. In some ways, new dungeons are more dangerous than the bigger ones that have been around for a while. You see, when I walked in, the door snapped shut and wouldn't open again. That happens with many of the small dungeons. We don't know why, but they like keeping people in more than the bigger ones do. At any rate, I did what my dad—your great-grandpa—always told me to do: 'When you find yourself in a situation that is beyond what you're used to, stop and think, assess what you have, and move forward.'

"Well, I don't remember everything I had with me, other than my work knife and my gathering bag, which I'd thought was going to be filled with leaves. What I do remember was that when I opened my lifebook, I had the option for a new class. What your dad told you about classes is mostly correct. However, there is a fourth way to get another class. It's just so rare that most people don't know about it, and it's definitely not worth mentioning in general conversation. This special class instance is to be the first sentient to enter a new dungeon.

"I was offered the ultra-rare class of pathfinder. It gave me the passive skill of magic sense, which lets me see how magic moves, the passive skill of decreased metabolic consumption, and a third passive skill of increased healing. I also got the active skill of dungeon safety. This allows me to create a twelve-hour bubble during which no one can get hurt, but only in the dungeon.

"I spent the next three months in the dungeon by myself, fighting my way through giant rats and spiders, bats that shot fire, little monsters that looked like a white-and-orange ball with a head that floated on top and just kind of hovered there. It was an adventure, all right. My business partner was not happy I was gone for so long. I'd only planned on being gone for the day, so I'd left my camp set up. When I got back, it was all gone. The only things that hadn't been stolen were inside my wagon."

Alexander leaned back in his chair, and Honor moved down to his lap and started to loudly purr as he petted her big head.

"Wow! Grandpa, I bet you got out with lots of loot after being in there so long!" Sinclair said.

Alexander gave a short, dry laugh. "Well, that's the thing about new dungeons. The first few times people go in, they don't get any loot. Don't know why, but I got out of there with a new class that I had leveled multiple times and a broken knife. I looked like a beggar, and by the time I found my way out, my clothes didn't fit because I'd lost so much fat. They looked like they had been chewed up by a Gorkle with all the fights I had been in."

Gretchen looked up at her grandpa from the floor and whispered, "Did you ever *go* back into *th*e dungeon?"

"Nope! That was the first and last time Alexander Bishop, the pathfinder, was ever in a dungeon. Not that I haven't been offered plenty of money to go in, but it's just not something I ever want to relive."

CHAPTER THREE

"Planning is important. It's how you know what to do. However, if that is all you do, then you might as well not plan."

—*Charles Bishop*

Charles smiled at his dad. "All right. Now, everyone, clear off your places, and then come back to the table for the morning meeting."

Once the table was wiped down, all the Bishops sat back down. This was a regular part of their day. After a time of prayer and reading the Scripture, Charles Bishop stood at the foot of the hewn log table with a large leather-bound book with a nasty-looking gouge on the top edge and started giving out instructions. "Okay, get your lifebooks out, and you will start to get your quests for the day." He opened his own book.

The children grabbed their left wrists with their right hands, and a small leather book appeared in each open left hand. Then, just as they did every morning, they turned to the *Active Quests* section of the book. Lifebooks were the interface for interacting with the world on Purvas, and they distinguished sapient races from animals. They mysteriously showed up when the third moon disappeared, and they caused a considerable amount of unrest as society adjusted to their existence. However, these days, their use was part of the normal function of society, as they allowed people to see which quests they were working on and what their skill levels were. The books even showed the experience points people had earned. Once a person turned fifteen years old, it showed their class as well. Generally speaking, kids on Purvas tended not to use lifebooks much because most of the features were inaccessible, but the Bishop parents made sure their kids were an exception to the rule.

"Now, Sinclair," their dad said, "as you can see, today, we need you to make sure the animal and garden chores are completed. You may assign out no more than three-fourths of the requirements to your siblings."

Sinclair looked at the leather lifebook in his hands. "I can see it in my quests, but it looks different from how it normally looks. It's showing that I can get double the experience by either doing it all or getting everyone to do it happily."

Their grandpa, still sitting in his rocking chair by the main hearth, said, "That seems like a first for you, in preparation for the selection of your class. Watch for things like that in the future, because many times, if you get all the extra objectives, you will get a huge windfall of experience points. Class quests can be like that as well."

Their dad nodded and looked at Penelope. “Okay, Pen. Today, you are in charge of lunch for the kids and dinner. We’ll have guests tonight, so I’ve assigned you a second quest to make dinner rolls. Your mom also would like you to help Ren work on his multiplication tables, which brings you up to three quests today.”

“How many guests are we having, and should I make the brown rolls or the butter rolls?” Pen asked.

“We’re having the Stoneheads over for dinner, so three additional helpings, and make the brown rolls. Gibbish likes those the best,” Mary replied.

“Oh, and, Pen, a stew is fine. We don’t need to be fancy with them. They’re close friends of your grandpa.” Charles added, turning to Ren, “Okay, for you, work with Penelope to learn your eight times table. Your second quest is to happily help with the chores if asked. Your third quest for the day is to move three of our dwarf chairs out of the barn and set them up at the table. We’ll need them for tonight.”

“Dad, should I get the ones with the armrests?” Warren asked.

“Get one with armrests. Put it at the end of the table and the other two to either side of it.” Clapping his hands together, their dad looked at Gretchen. “Okay, last set of quests. Your mom has left the books for the store here. Go through and balance them. Your second quest is to help Sinclair if he asks, and your third is to get the good dishes out for dinner tonight."

"Dad, wi*th th*e books, am I doing *th*e yearly full balance or just *th*e monthly?" Gretchen asked.

"Just do the monthly. Your mom will help you with the yearly next week when we get back to the store. We want to make sure we're ready when the tax collectors come by to look at our books," Charles said with a sigh.

Grandpa Bishop spoke up. "Kids, us adults need to go into town today to get some things. We will be back in the afternoon, and no, you can't come."

"Are you getting Slair's birthday gifts?" Gretchen asked excitedly.

Grandpa Bishop gave Gretchen a quick wink and appeared to ignore her question. "It might be good if you can pull some hay out of the barn for us too. The weather looks like it might turn colder today." He gently pushed the cat from his lap and stood up.

As he was heading to his curtained-off room, Gretchen quickly came over to him and whispered, "Papa, *c*an you pick up some of *th*e peppermint *c*andy *th*at I like when you go into town and maybe get Slair a new belt from me too? I have money." She passed a few copper coins to her grandpa.

"Don't you think your parents would be better at getting him a belt than I would?"

"Maybe, but they wouldn't *g*et me any *c*andy and would tell me to save my money."

"I'll see what I can do," he said with a wink.

Not half an hour later, the older family members were on their way out the door. Just as they were about to leave, Mary turned back. "Sinclair, I am so proud of you and everything you have done and how you have grown." She gave him an awkwardly long hug. Then she hugged the other kids.

Before she could turn to open the door, Honor looked right at her and meowed. Mary got a thoughtful look on her face. "Sinclair, since it's getting colder, try to keep Honor in the house. We want to keep her warm."

Grandpa Bishop started to laugh. "Like anyone could keep that cat in if she didn't want to stay."

"Don't worry too much about the cat," their dad said. "Just get your chores done and get things ready for dinner. We'll be back as soon as we can. We just have to grab a few things from your grandpa's shop."

Chapter Four

"I have never seen a more successful business than one that has a cat nearby. It's as if they bring good luck or something. I've also never seen a more scratched face than that of a dwarven engineer who tried to give a cat a bath."

—Rikwast, chief foreman, second division, Royal Engineers for King Edward V - Two Sisters 1139

After the adults left, Penelope spoke up. "Well, we have quests to do, and like it or not, they don't get any easier if we put them off, so let's get to work!"

"I guess," said Sinclair. His sister was bossy, but her logic was sound, so he opened his lifebook again to make it look like he was getting ready to work.

- *Pick the totatoes and charrots.**
- *Gather the eggs.*
- *Feed and walk the horse.*
- *Muck the stalls.*

* No one on Purvas knows exactly where totatoes and charrots came from. The story is that a bag of seeds just showed up in someone's cupboard one day and that someone was either brave or foolish enough to plant the unknown seeds in their garden. Whatever the case, the soil seemed to be perfect, and they were sold to the upper class as a "rare, otherworldly delicacy" even though they basically tasted like potatoes and carrots.

*****Double experience points available*****

** Diligence - do all the tasks by yourself in the time allotted.*

** Leadership - convince others to cheerfully help you.*

Sinclair sighed. He had a choice to make—he could either do the tasks by himself or convince the others to help him. Since he didn't feel like doing everything by himself, he decided to see if he could persuade his siblings to help him with the list.

"All right, you guys. I really want to get these bonus experience points, so I need you all to help me with my jobs. I think it will be cool to see what happens, and it's almost my birthday, so you should help me. Here's a list of what needs to be done."

"I'll get the totatoes and charrots," Penelope grumbled. She wasn't excited about the idea of helping her brother, but he did play the birthday-boy card, and she was kind of curious to see what would happen with the bonus points since she was only a year away.

"I'll fee*d* and walk *th*e hor*s*e," Gretchen volunteered. She loved spending time with horses, so it was a task that she was happy to do, especially if it meant taking a little more time to get to the accounting.

"I get to gather the eggs!" yelled Warren as he jumped up, scaring Honor off her perch near the window.

"No, Warren, I was thinking you should muck out the stalls because it's my birthday," Sinclair said.

"*What?*" said Warren. "That's the hardest job. You should do it."

The *Bonus Points* section in Sinclair's lifebook started flashing. He knew he needed to turn things around quickly, but he didn't want to muck out the stalls either. Then the idea hit him.

"I know—I'll race you for it. Last one to the barn has to muck out the stalls!" Sinclair hollered as he jumped from his log chair.

He threw open the back door and started to run toward the barn. Next came Penelope and then Gretchen busting out the back. The last to leave was Warren. Being the youngest, he was already at a disadvantage with his short legs. He also wasn't very careful, so when he slammed the door shut on his way out, it bounced back open.

Not three seconds later, Sinclair saw, out of the corner of his eye, a brownish-gray Maine coon. He turned fully and found that Honor was making a break for the woods. Sinclair changed direction and pointed to where Honor was going.

"Honor got out! Get her!" he yelled, running at full speed.

Honor crouched down and froze for a second as she made eye contact with Sinclair. Then she darted between two large trees and into the woods. As the kids reached the woods, they slowed down. In front of them was a brick path that they'd never seen before, even though they'd been coming to their grandparents' house once or twice a year their entire lives. Despite its unfamiliarity, the bricks were old and showed signs of care and weather as if they had been there for decades.

Warren pointed ahead of them and yelled, "She stopped! Get her!"

The kids darted down the path toward Honor, who was lying in a ray of sun about twenty feet away. She rolled on her back and stretched. They'd almost caught her when she snapped upright and jumped at a bird that flew out of a bush. Then she was off again, chasing the bird down the path.

The children followed, never getting closer than six feet but never farther than twenty feet away. Every time they lagged behind, the cat would find something to sniff or a place to lie down. When they got closer, she would find a bug to chase. At last, they came to an opening in the woods, and before them was a large old barn.

Looking like she knew just where to go, Honor ran for a loose board in the wall of the old barn. She slowed to a walk and almost pranced through the opening, sparing only one look over her shoulder to see that yes, the kids were coming.

The Bishop children reached the barn and stopped. They'd never seen this barn before, which was kind of odd since it had a well-worn path and they'd spent years playing on the farm. It was old, so they guessed that it might be dangerous to go into. The thatched roof was overgrown and even had a bush growing out of it, and the boards were gray though not quite ramshackle.

"Honor went in there, so we need to get her, but I'm not sure how safe that barn is. I'm going to be the one that goes in." Sinclair turned to face everyone else.

"We can't go in wiffout Dad! It's all dark and scary," Gretchen whined.

"Well, *someone* let Honor out, and since I'm the oldest, I'm going to go in." Sinclair cast an aggravated look at Warren.

"I didn't mean to let her out. It's not my fault the door bounced open," Warren moaned as he looked at the ground.

"If you are going in there, you likely need a light, so let's get you a lantern." Penelope turned, grabbed her skirt midway, and pulled it up so that she could walk faster then headed back toward, the house, calling over her shoulder, "Warren, grab a towel so when we find her, we can wrap her up. Gretchen, stay here and make sure she doesn't come out. Sinclair, take a look around and make sure there isn't another hole. No sense in chasing her in if she just runs out again."

Sinclair looked at the other two, and the siblings came to an unspoken agreement that their sister's plan made sense. As Warren ran toward the house and Sinclair started around the barn, Gretchen stood near the barn and watched the hole. In less than ten minutes, Penelope and Warren were back with their items.

"Did you close the door this time?" Penelope snipped.

"Yes," Warren snapped back. This was a big mess, and he was already feeling guilty, but Sinclair was clearly wrong, too, since he didn't want to muck out the stalls and tried to pass his hardest chore off on everyone else. *Why is Penelope so hard on me?* he thought. *Who made her boss, anyways?*

Sinclair came around the front of the barn. "Well, if there is another way out, I sure couldn't find it. This barn seems to be completely closed off. Hand me the lantern so I can go get her out."

"Be careful—we don't know what is in there or why Grandpa has the barn closed off." Penelope gave her brother the lantern. "We can only guess it is because it's not safe to be in there, but it might not just be the building that isn't safe. There might be old tools, so watch your step."

Sinclair laughed and said sarcastically, "Maybe Grandpa has his own dungeon here and this is the entrance!" Then he slid the lantern through the hole and followed his light into the closed-off barn.

CHAPTER FIVE

"Cats are smart. Have you ever seen one on a gnomish airship? They also don't like baths. Just don't do it—trust me."

—Gabrid Flintback, chief foreman, first division, Royal Engineers for King Edward V - Two Sisters 1139

The three kids on the outside watched the hole, listening for any clue of what was going on. They heard nothing from inside the barn—no sounds of things falling or people running around or any indication Sinclair was chasing a cat. All of the sudden, the plank pushed open, and Sinclair's beaming face appeared on the other side of the hole. "Guys, I'm going to need your help in here to find her, and you are not going to believe what is in here." He smiled.

"Well, what is it?" said Penelope.

"Just come in and see. I have no idea why we never knew about it. It is the coolest thing ever!"

"Fine! I thought this might happen," huffed Penelope as she reached into her dress pocket and pulled out three small lightstones. "I know that they don't give much light, but they're better than walking around with rushlights."

"Where did you get lightstones from?" Warren reached for the magical rock.

"Dad had a few in our travel packs. I thought they would be better than open flames in an old building." Penelope went over to the hole and ducked into the barn.

Warren and Gretchen followed quickly. In the middle of the barn was a huge green wagon with red trim and yellow accents. Even in the dim light, they could tell the paint was chipping. The wagon stood at least twelve feet tall and about ten feet wide. Most astoundingly, it was no less than twenty feet long, maybe even thirty. It was a beautiful closed-in wagon with doors and round windows built on giant iron-trimmed wheels. You could almost mistake it for a little house.

From where the children stood, they could see that the back of the wagon had a small porch with swing-down steps leading up to it. The porch was just large enough for two old wooden chairs painted bright red with yellow trim, and a door in the middle of the porch led into the wagon.

"Wow!" Warren yelled as he ran up to the door and stepped in. "This is amazing! Look at the cabinets and counter!"

"'Low down!" Gretchen called. "We haff to be careful not to break anyfing, and we're looking for Honor!"

As the girls went inside, a meow came from deep within the wagon. Sinclair went to another door at the right front and entered the wagon.

"Close the wagon doors! We don't want her to get out before we get her," Penelope said as she shut the back door.

The three youngest children ran into each other as they walked into the next part of the wagon, which was only about eight feet long and was a very tight squeeze. There was only one small walkway that even Warren had to turn sideways to get through. The rest of this room was all sets of shelves pushed up next to each other so tightly that you couldn't see between them.

***

Sinclair, meanwhile, was passing through a different room. The front of the wagon had four small built-in beds going up one wall, and on the other wall, four chairs hung from pegs in front of what looked like a table that could fold down into the space. There was also a large built-in chest of drawers with a cutout for a window. On the shelf in front of the window was a wooden box with a pretty pillow. Sitting on top of the pillow was Honor, who was purring.

"I have you now!" roared Sinclair as he moved in with the towel held wide.

Honor twitched her tail and jumped from her box onto one of the beds. She looked at Sinclair, turned, and launched herself out of the bed and through a trapdoor on the ceiling.

"She went on the roof!" Sinclair yelled as he grabbed a chair off the wall so that he could reach the opening. As he stood on the chair and started to grab the edge of the opening, he saw a built-in ladder that pulled down, so he used that instead to scramble up.

On the roof, Sinclair saw a driver's bench big enough for two people to sit on. He also saw Honor purring as she pushed her face and body up against a large wooden brake handle. The handle moved forward, and the wagon shifted. Then she looked at Sinclair, jumped back through the trap door, and landed on the wagon floor.

Sinclair scrambled down the ladder again as his siblings came into the bed compartment. He closed the trapdoor and shot an angry smile at Honor, who had climbed back up to the pillow. "Now you truly have no place to go!" he said as he stalked toward her.

Honor meowed, curled up, and began purring in response to his declaration. As she did, bright blue and pink light started to flash through the windows on both sides of the room, and there was a loud rumbling like wagon wheels on a cobblestone road and a whooshing similar to the sound you would hear when you were being pushed too fast and too hard on a swing. The whole wagon lurched and shuddered. The next thing they heard was water hitting the windows, like rain in a hard storm, which transitioned to more lights and finally resolved with a gentle rocking motion. As the light from the windows stopped flashing and the commotion settled, the windows gently opened, and daylight poured in through the gaps in the drawn curtains.

CHAPTER SIX

"Take the time to hug family, even if you're angry with them right now. You never know when you'll see them again."

—Grandpa Bishop

When the lights stopped, the children got the familiar feeling of their quests failing as the information updates started pouring in. Warren opened his lifebook to find that two of his quests were marked as failed. While he wasn't particularly excited about moving the chairs or helping with the chores, he didn't enjoy seeing them archived into the *Failed Quests* section. Warren was no stranger to failed quests. They weren't something he hoped for, and they normally came with consequences, but they weren't the end of the world. However, he was a stranger to the red number that appeared in the top margin of his page.

"Eighteen hours!" Warren yelled, jumping up and down. His lifebook clearly had the red number as well. "Do you see that? I have a countdown! I can't believe I have a countdown!"

Countdowns were something Sinclair had heard of but never experienced. They typically appeared when a classed individual got a quest with a time limit, so the adventurers in his parents' store would sometimes be in a hurry and grumpy if they were running out of time.

"I do too," Gretchen chirped.

"I see the countdown, as well, but while it's fun and slightly disturbing, I'm more concerned about the light outside and what must have just happened," Penelope replied in a dignified, motherly sort of way.

Sinclair moved to the door and opened it, and light streamed in. They were no longer in the barn, which was both exciting and highly worrisome. The Bishops stepped outside and closed the doors to keep Honor inside. She wasn't planning on following them this time, since she had her box with a pillow next to a window, but considering what had just happened, it was a logical step for the children to take.

As they walked around the wagon, they looked at the area, trying to figure out where they were. They'd arrived in a clearing that looked like it had at one time been a well-used campsite. There were more than a dozen fire rings made of stone, with logs that had long since rotted around each ring. The road still looked like it was in use because there were ruts in the dirt, but there was no one to be seen.

***

It only took the children a few minutes to realize that they were not near their grandparents' home any longer. The trees were the wrong type, and the air was warmer. Alarmingly, they couldn't see any path that the wagon would have taken when it rolled from the barn—which was also missing.

The children almost simultaneously came to the same conclusion—that they were lost—and rather than panic, decided to fight instead.

Penelope yelled, "Why did you have to call us into the barn? If you hadn't done that, this wouldn't have happened, and we would still be at Papa's house! Now we're in the middle of nowhere!"

"Oh, that's rich!" Sinclair yelled back. "If you didn't want to come into the barn, you didn't have to, but it was Warren who opened the door to the wagon. If he hadn't done that, we would still be outside it."

"We would have gone in one way or the other. There was nothing in there but the wagon," Warren whined.

"Well, if you hadn't been so set on getting Honor back that you were willing to go into the strange barn, we wouldn't be here," Penelope snapped back.

Sinclair was pacing around and waving his hands. "I was just trying to cover for Warren's mistake again! If it hadn't been for him slamming the door and not closing it right, Honor wouldn't have gotten out of the house, and I wouldn't have had to try to figure out how to get her back in!"

"Hey! I just didn't want to muck out the stable." Pouting, Warren fell to the ground, sat crossed-legged, and started to cry. "I didn't know the door would bounce open and the cat would get out, and besides, Dad said not to worry if Honor got out. You were the one who told us to chase her!"

"Mom and Dad always leave you in charge, so it was your responsibility to get the door closed, so don't try to blame this on Warren!" Penelope yelled. "And he's right—we were told not to worry about Honor! You're always trying to shift the blame. You know full well we're in this mess because of you."

"Sure—blame it on me. You were the one that got the lantern and the towel. If you hadn't, I wouldn't have been able to go in and see the wagon, so it's your fault," Sinclair said lamely, still waving his hands around and looking up at the sky.

"'Top it! Just *'top it*, you two!" Gretchen yelled. "We don't know where we are, and you're out here yelling, which makes *no* sense!" She lowered her voice. "We don't know where to get food or where home is or where we can sleep or anyfing, and you were yelling so much dat Warren ran into duh woods." Gretchen started crying as she pointed to a path in the woods that looked ominously abandoned.

"Great, just what we need—Warren running off again! I'll go get him. You two, stay here near the wagon so I can call for you and get back." Sinclair sprinted toward the woods.

With Sinclair going to find their brother, the two girls calmed down and started to gather things that would be helpful just like they had been taught to do when traveling. As they walked near the edge of the clearing, looking for firewood, they noticed the odd fact that one of the fire rings seemed to be perfectly designed for their wagon. They found it even stranger that the wagon had managed to stop in the exact place that seemed logical for their location—perfectly spaced from the campfire and situated nicely in the clearing—but since they were lost, they didn't put too much thought into it.

Chapter Seven

"Brothers are great! They yell at each other all the time but stand up for each other when someone else picks on them. Wish I had one. All I have is a pet rabbit, and it never talks with me."

—*Fenwich Mashwalker, captain of the gnomish airship* Gearwind - *1149*

Warren had had enough. His brother and sister were fighting again, and while it was not common, it happened more when they thought they were in trouble. So Warren did what he tended to do—he ran. He knew where the wagon was, so he decided to poke around the trees and see what he could find.

It was always better to be in the woods than to be around people but even more so when his siblings were fighting. If Warren had stayed, Sinclair would keep trying to blame him for the whole mess when everyone could tell it was Sinclair's fault they were not at the farm.

Warren had spent lots of time playing in the woods, so knew he could find his way back. That was one of the things he prided himself on—he could always get back home no matter what. As he ran, he remembered the time he'd spent a whole day in the woods near his parents' house and found a little cave to play in. It was a nice peaceful spot with a waterfall close by. Later, he discovered that a bear lived in the cave and had been out that day. The experience shook him up a bit, but Warren had learned what animal dens looked like, so of course, he wouldn't make that mistake again.

As he meandered, he stopped feeling sad and started to get mad. If things went the way they tended to go, Sinclair would come out into the woods to find him and tell Warren what a big bother he was and how he was a baby for running off and how it was all his fault that they were not at the farm. Maybe this time, he could teach Sinclair a lesson.

He thought about all the times he'd failed to get Sinclair. It always seemed that when they got into a fistfight, Sinclair would win, and then Warren would have to say Sinclair was right. Or Sinclair would sit on him or squeeze him until Warren agreed with him. If they were going to get in trouble about something, he would be forced to take the blame. Sometimes, he was able to get a lucky hit in or ambush Sinclair and give him a few good punches. The outcome would still be the same—Warren would lose, and it would be his fault—but it was worth the effort to try.

Warren looked around to find a stick he could use as a club and a place just far enough away that the girls wouldn't see what happened. He could always get Penelope and Gretchen to side with him if he told them Sinclair had started it. It was his parents whom he couldn't always convince, and the last time he'd tried to get them on his side, things had turned out worse than they would have if he had just accepted all responsibility.

Before long, Warren found a branch big enough to make a club out of. It looked dead on the tree. He started to bend it back and forth, putting his whole body into the movement. As he worked on the branch, it slipped from his grip and sprang back and hit him in the face, busting his top lip open.

Hot tears streamed down his face as he sucked on his lip as he stood back up to keep working on the branch. While he was crying from the pain, he was also a weirdly happy about the busted lip. His sisters would side with him, and Slair wouldn't stand a chance—he would be the one to blame about this whole mess when they got home.

Just as the branch was breaking off, Sinclair found him. "Warren, drop the branch and come back to the wagon. You know how dumb it is to be out here by yourself. No telling what's around!" Sinclair shouted at his brother as he came through the trees.

Warren turned with the branch in his hand, blood dripping down his face, and smiled. Then he dropped the smile and stared, horrified. "Slair, behind you," Warren barely eked out.

"Stop trying to trick me. Drop the stick and come home. I'm not falling for another one of your dumb ambushes. Every time I come to find you, you try to trick me. Now, stop it all and come back!"

"Boar! Behind you!" Warren yelled as he turned and ran, dropping the stick.

***

Sinclair looked behind him and saw a small adult boar with two seven-inch tusks. It was no more than ten feet away and looking right at him. Sinclair tried to back away, keeping his eyes on the beast. As the boar looked at him, it stamped its front right hoof, and a splash of green light shot out from it.

Sinclair chose that moment to make a break for it and run for all he was worth. As he sprinted away, he heard the boar behind him, breaking through the underbrush. He jumped as high as he could over a fallen tree, which he cleared easily, but the boar decided to plow through it, sending rotten wood everywhere. When Sinclair glanced back, he saw that the whole boar was glowing green.

Sinclair cut sharply to his left and started to run around big trees as best he could, with the boar just behind him. It appeared that the creature could bust through the dead trees but went around living ones. Sinclair was glancing behind him when he found a slope the hard way—his feet lost the ground, and he went down. The incline was steep and went down about ten feet. He skinned his legs as he tumbled.

When he reached the bottom, he looked up and saw the boar stamping its foot, glaring at him. It backed out of his line of sight and snorted. Then the boar headed down into the ravine with a crash. It stumbled and seemed to have trouble staying upright. Sinclair lost no time and started to run away again, searching for a way to scramble back up.

He soon found a tree that had fallen over, and he used the branches to move upward. As he pulled himself out of the ravine, he saw that the boar had gotten to its feet and was walking the other way, as if it was out for a nice stroll and hadn't just tried to run him down.

Sinclair looked around, trying to figure out where he was. He knew he was lost, as he wasn't even sure which side of the ravine he should be on, let alone the way back to the wagon or Warren. He started to get mad. If Warren hadn't run off, Sinclair wouldn't have gotten a skinned-up leg and torn britches. Yet another thing that Warren had messed up.

Sinclair wandered around and was trying to figure out where he was when he saw the boar again. Its head was down, and it was eating some mushrooms growing in the ground. Sinclair slowly moved back and around, trying to keep an eye on the boar without getting too close. He was near a huge oak tree when he heard his brother.

"Up here, Slair! The low branch is on the other side!"

Sinclair tore around the giant tree to see a branch several feet thick that was almost touching the ground. He scrambled up it just as the boar passed under him. It seemed like the boar had been aware of where he was the whole time and was just waiting for Sinclair to turn his back.

Warren waved Sinclair over to where the trunk split and there was a large landing of sorts. "We should be safe up here. That green glow should be the boar's plow-through attack and only works on wood that's no more than two inches in diameter. The adventurers say if you're getting chased by one, you should climb the biggest tree you can." Warren looked down at the boar. "Think we'll be up here long?"

"No telling, Ren. I thought I lost it in a ravine just back that way a bit," Sinclair said, trying to catch his breath.

"Oh, that one is still there—this is the other one," Warren said with a big grin. "This one is bigger too!"

"Great. You run off, and we get stuck in a tree with leveled boars after us."

"Could be worse."

"How do you figure?" Sinclair rolled his eyes.

Warren smiled and cocked his head at his brother. "They could be fire boars and not just normal ones—they could burn down the tree we're in. Or we could still be down there. So lots of ways it could be worse."

The two boys were quiet for a bit and watched the boars as they met back up and started to graze again. After about twenty minutes, the animals moved off, and the boys dropped back down to the ground.

"So, what are we going to tell the girls?" Ren asked.

"Let's not tell them about getting chased by leveled boars. No need to scare them."

"So what do we tell them about your leg?"

"The truth—I fell down a ravine."

"Fair enough. No boars."

"Yup, no boars, no big tree. You know that Gretchen would want to come and climb it."

The boys walked back with Warren in the lead, not talking anymore. They were both tired and still hadn't solved their problems, but at least they were done with their argument for the moment.

Chapter Eight

"Did you know that if you set two fire rocks next to each other, they'll catch flame?"

—Warren every single time Sinclair made a fire on the last family camping trip

The boys had been gone for over an hour when they finally returned to the campsite. Under normal circumstances, their mother would have scolded them for being so dirty and disheveled. Both looked like they'd been angry, but much of their animosity toward each other seemed to have been worked out in the standard boy fashion. Warren had a split lip, and Sinclair had a scraped-up, bruised leg and a tear in his pants. Since their mother was not with them, their sisters were happy to fill in for her.

"Did you two fig*ht* again?" Gretchen asked them as they approached.

"None of your business," Warren mumbled.

"Yes, it is our business. You are our brothers, and we're not at home, so we need to stick together," Penelope said.

"No! I was running when I fell down a ditch and busted my leg. I have no idea how he got the fat lip, but he had it when I found him."

Sinclair huffed and sat down near the fire ring. "What we really need to do is figure out what's going on," he said in his best dad voice. "Countdown timers show up when important things are happening. I thought they always generated a quest, but since I don't see a new one in my lifebook, that's the theory we're going with for now. We need to break up and do our normal camping chores to get ready for the night."

Penelope sighed. "You're right. We have wood for a fire, but I'm not sure how we're going to start it. While you boys were gone, I found berries and nuts that we can have for lunch."

"*You* found *th*e berries and nuts? Don't you mean *we* found them—or even more accurately, I found *th*em?" asked Gretchen.

Penelope rolled her eyes and shrugged. "Well, when you put it that way, yes. Gretchen and I picked them while you guys were out playing in the woods and being ridiculous. We even had to get the wood ourselves, which is *your* job, Sinclair, because we weren't sure when you would be back. You're lucky you have us around. Now, stop ruining our lives and go ahead and get started figuring out how to start the fire."

Sinclair glanced at Warren as the brothers tried not to laugh. Penelope always had a flare for drama. "Sure. I'm going to see if there's anything in the wagon that can help start a fire. Otherwise, it might be a cold night." Sinclair headed toward the wagon. He was good at building fires, but that didn't mean he was excited about trying to start a fire from scratch.

Penelope turned to Warren. "So, how did you get a fat lip?"

Warren rolled his eyes. "I tried to break off a branch so that I could hit Sinclair with it because I was mad, but it didn't break and bounced back and hit me."

A few minutes later, Sinclair returned with a small bag that held a piece of flint and a sheathed knife. He sat down and got to work on the fire. Warren went into the wagon, as well, and curled up on his bunk. Honor jumped down from her perch and started to rub her head under his chin.

"Honor, I'm glad we found you, but they all hate me for letting you out of the house. Why did you have to get out?" he whined.

Honor just purred and let him pet her soft fur even though he was holding her a bit too tightly.

***

While Sinclair and Penelope were busy trying to get the fire started, Gretchen took the time to search for more berries and other things to eat. They spent a few nights every year camping on their way to their papa's house, and they'd been taught what they could eat and where to find it. Part of the fun of the trips was seeing how much they could find while moving.

As she went about her tasks, she couldn't stop thinking about what was going on. *Papa has a magical wagon that he kept locked up? Where are we? Was this how he got his start? He's never talked about his early days of business before—he's only said that once he met Grandma, he just had to open a store in Cnoc. What else have they been keeping from us?*

Dad had moved from Cnoc to Heuvel to open his shop and had met Mom there. They ran a very successful adventure-supply shop, selling to all the brave travelers who came through town on their way to exploring and fighting with monsters in the dungeon nearby. Gretchen enjoyed meeting them and hearing all their exciting stories. Adventurers were from many different races, so it was neat to hear what strategies and plans an elf or a halfling would use compared to someone big like an orc or half giant.

As she mused and gathered berries, she came across some of the most beautiful wildflowers she had ever seen and stopped to pick them. When she had enough, she made them into a necklace and a bracelet and then put some in her hair. Despite her being lost, the forest was relaxing, and she soon forgot most of her worries. One thing led to the next, and before she knew it, she found herself in front of a tree with bees coming in and out of it.

***

Sinclair almost had the fire going when he heard Gretchen yell, "Tinclair, help! Tum quick! I need you!"

Remembering the wild boar they had met, he dropped everything and came running across the through the brush toward Gretchen. Penelope dropped the berries she'd been gathering in the apron of her skirt and came running as well. When they arrived, they found Gretchen smiling, pointing to the tree.

"Tinclair, help me get duh honey! You helped Dad get honey, so you haff to get it for us now!" Gretchen jumped up and down.

Sinclair caught his breath, placing his hands on his knees. "You're okay? You yelled for help in the middle of nowhere, and you are okay?" he asked incredulously.

"Yes, I'm fine. I just wanted you to get me the honey so that we could have something sweet."

"But we are out in the middle of nowhere, and you *yelled*," he said, drawing out the last word. "I thought you were hurt or in trouble, not that you wanted honey."

Gretchen quickly realized her mistake. "I am *s*orry, *S*inclair. I shouldn't have yelled for help. I wasn't thinking about that. I just wanted honey. Will you forgive me for scaring you?" she asked softly.

"Yes, I forgive you. I can't stay mad at you for long, and you know that."

"Does that mean you'll get the honey?" Gretchen replied.

"I can't even think about honey right now until I get the fire going. Which I almost had until you yelled." He turned and walked back toward the firepit.

"Gretchen, please come and help me pick up all the berries I dropped when I ran over here to see if you were hurt," Penelope said tersely.

"Okay, Pen, I can help. Sorry *th*at I scared you two."

"That's okay. I want honey too. It just isn't something I think we can get right now." Penelope hugged her little sister. "Let's finish getting the meal ready and go check on Warren. He's been in the wagon by himself long enough to calm down."

***

That night, the kids sat around the fire, eating the things that they'd found. They had berries and nuts and some leaves they knew were safe to eat. Gretchen had even found mint, which they made into tea. They didn't get the honey because they had no place to put it, and the special hat that their dad had to help keep the bees away was back at home. In the wagon, they'd found needle and thread to fix Sinclair's pants, four wooden sets of dishes, and a large metal pot. As they ate dinner and drank their tea, they talked about what was happening.

"Well, we're in a tight spot—there's no doubt about that. We have this wagon that brought us here, but we don't know where *here* is, so we don't know if we can get home." Sinclair sighed deeply, the way his dad did when he was talking about problems. "We really need to stick together and not wander off, and we need to work together. We don't have much food, and we can only guess what the countdown is for. Winter is going to be here soon, which means even though it's warmer here, we need to get ready for a spot of cold."

The children sat in silence for a few minutes, thinking. Penelope was the first to break the quiet. "I found some paper and a few pencils in the wagon. I can make a list of everything we have and everything we need and everything we can find. Then I can make checklists for everyone so we make sure we're getting the most done."

Sinclair rolled his eyes. Though the darkness hid the action, his tone conveyed the same feeling. "Pen, the lists will be helpful, but we don't need checklists. We can just do what we need to do, and if we need a reminder, we can just note it in our lifebooks."

"Checklists help with everything," Penelope said. "They would keep us on task and doing the next thing. They're how I get so much done! That, and you can only put notes in for active quests. You know that."

"Well, then, you can make one for yourself, but don't feel the need to make it for me," Sinclair volleyed back.

"Now, as I was saying, we need to stay together and work together, so I guess I need to do this as well." Sinclair stood up and walked over to Warren. He squatted down beside his kid brother. "Warren, please forgive me for blaming you for this whole mess we're in. We all should have been more careful about the door."

Warren cocked his head and smiled from ear to ear. "I forgive you. I still think it wasn't my fault. She's always been in and out of the house, and Mom told you to keep her in, not me."

"I don't know what will happen when the countdown gets to zero, but we should all sleep in the wagon tonight in case it moves again. I'm sure that would wake us up," Gretchen said.

As the Bishops were putting out the fire, a chirping meow came from the woods. They turned to see Honor moving into the fire ring with a bird in her mouth. She lay down and started to eat it in the firelight, purring happily.

"Who let Honor out?" cried Warren as he jumped up and wrapped his arms around the cat.

"She was inside asleep when I got Warren for dinner," Gretchen said, eying the cat, who had just dropped her bird after being roughly picked up.

"Maybe we missed a door or window. We should look around. We don't want to lose her here of all places," Sinclair added.

The children made their way into the wagon. All the doors were closed, and the windows were too. Penelope said, "She must have slipped out when we weren't looking. We just have to do a better job of watching her."

CHAPTER NINE

"Classes are great, but they built the locks at Kalva without them!"

—*Gnomish saying*

The Bishop children were rudely awakened in the morning as the whole wagon shook and flashing bright-blue and pink light poured in through the windows. The screeching and rhythmic thumping made them brace for impact as they felt the wagon about to break an axel on cobblestone.

Sinclair got thrown off the top bunk and hit the ground with an "Oof." He sat up and rubbed his shoulder. "Well, I guess we know what the countdown was for now."

By that time, everyone was awake and starting to get out of bed except for Honor, who was still curled up on the fluffy pillow in her box by her window. The kids opened the door to see the morning light peeking over the trees. Sadness passed over them as they saw that they were once again in the middle of nowhere.

Warren was the first one out of the wagon. He circled around to check his surroundings and was met with a delightful sight. "Guys, there's a town! And it's big enough to have a wall!"

The others came running out, and the celebration broke loose as they jumped and hugged each other as if they had never expected to see another town again in their whole lives after one day of being completely lost. The town was about a mile away. It sat on a hill, and dawn was breaking behind it, silhouetting the small skyline and casting shadows on the slope. As their eyes traveled down the road, they could see smoke from the chimneys rising over the palisade walls that circled the little town, with a gate wide enough for two wagons to pass each other.

Looking around the landscape, the children noticed that the whole area was rolling hills covered in a beautiful array of farmers' fields and pastures. Even in the early light, the children could see grazing flocks of sheep and the shepherds who tended them. The road they were near was lined with a low stacked-stone wall, and not too far off were dug-out homes like what halflings tended to favor.

After taking in the situation, Sinclair said, "Okay, let's figure out what we're doing today so we can make a plan. Like Dad says, 'Failing to plan...'"

"'Is planning to fail,'" the kids chimed in with a slight groan.

Sinclair smiled. "Right! So back in the wagon, and we'll have a quick meeting and then find out where we are and what's going on."

The kids headed back into the wagon, following Sinclair. They knew that he was right about needing a plan, as they made one every day with their dad back home. When they got to the small table in the wagon, Honor was peering out the window and twitching her tail. Warren pulled his chair over, stood on it, and looked outside. Outside the wagon was a nice brown bunny.

He smiled and petted Honor. "You can't have that rabbit—you're inside, and it's out there. There's no way for you to get around the wagon without it seeing you."

Then he took his chair back to the table and opened his lifebook. The rest were all smiling at Honor as well. Soon, they all had their lifebooks open. A new countdown said *4 Days* in the top margin of every page.

Sinclair stood at his spot and looked at each of the kids. He tried not to look worried and put his hands on the back of the chair just like his dad would do. Then he cleared his throat and started into the meeting.

"Well, I guess since Dad's not here, that puts me in charge. The way I see it, we need to find out where we are and then make some plans. That being said, since it looks like we're in this town for the next four days, we should all try to find some work, at least for today. We don't have any money, and we need food, so coin will come in handy, especially if we want to go home. We won't know how much we need until we have more information, but anything is a start."

Penelope said, "I guess you kind of are in charge, but you can't give us quests until you get a class. So we all need to remember what we're doing. Since we can't put notes in our lifebooks for nonquest things, we should make a list of what we need to do."

Gretchen rolled her eyes. "Seriously, Pen? It's two *th*ings. We need to learn where we are and find some day jobs to get money for foo*d*. Maybe we need to do other *th*ings later, but it's kind of easy to remember."

Warren passed a small notebook and a pencil to Penelope. "Here. You can use this for your list, but I know I'll be fine. We need to find out where we are and get food."

Penelope gave Warren a warm smile. She quickly opened the old notebook and started to make her checklist for the day.

Sinclair smirked. "Okay, so we all know what we need to do. Let's go figure out what's going on."

Gretchen smiled at Sinclair. "*Th*ere's one other *th*ing we need to *th*ink about."

"What?" asked Warren.

"It's Slair's fifteen*th* bir*th*day, and we don't have any*th*ing to give him." Gretchen looked at Penelope and Warren.

Sinclair gave a tight, pained smile. Tradition had it that on his fifteenth birthday, he would receive some nice gifts and get to look at his class options. But his parents weren't there, and his siblings had brought nothing with them, so there weren't going to be any gifts or any adults to help walk him through class selection—not a fun day for a birthday. But he needed to be strong for his brother and sisters.

"That's okay. We have more important things to think about than my birthday, like getting home," Sinclair said stiffly.

As the kids walked outside, they saw Honor near the door to the wagon, happily eating a rabbit that she'd been watching earlier. The siblings stopped and looked at each other, almost daring each other to explain what had happened.

Sinclair mumbled, "Umm... let's go. We can talk about that on the way."

"Right," the other kids said as they headed to town.

Warren looked back at a very proud and happy Honor. "How did she get out?"

CHAPTER TEN

"Doing is important. Doing right is even more important. You can save yourself lots of grief if you do your tasks right the first time."

—Charles Bishop to Sinclair after the third time in an hour he sent his son to sweep the store

They hiked the mile or so to the town, tossing out ideas about where they were and how to get home.

"Maybe we can buy several oxen and take *th*e wagon back to Grandpa," Gretchen suggested.

"Or if it isn't too far, we could just walk home. We can sleep under the trees. Nothing much will attack if we stay by the road," Penelope said.

"Those are both good ideas. I think we're likely far enough away that we would need to join a wagon caravan to get home," Sinclair said.

"We could see if there are giant birds around that we could pay to take us home. I always wanted to fly, and some of the birds are super nice," Warren happily said. "Or maybe we could find a dragon who could fly us home!"

"Ren, dragons would cost too much, and the birds hardly ever talk with people since they don't need much from us," Sinclair replied.

"Well, *th*ere was that one adventurer in *th*e gray robe with *th*at halfling rogue that said they flew wi*th* the giant birds before," Gretchen said. "You remember *th*em—they came in right before they headed off to the Heuvel dungeon."

"Yes, but they're the only ones, and I'm not sure they ever came out of the dungeon either— they at least didn't sell anything back to us," Penelope said.

Soon, they drew near to the town, which was about as large as their hometown of Heuvel. The homes were a mix of stone and wood. Most of the roofs appeared to be thatched, but a few that had clay shingles or wooden shakes. The road into the town was cobbled starting just a few feet from the palisade gate, which was still closed for the night. A short line of people was forming nearby, waiting for it to open.

The Bishops joined the line behind a few handcarts with produce and a wagon piled high with wool. Many of the people were waiting with small baskets as though this was something they did every day. Most stood very quietly as if they were still half-asleep. Cutting through the sleepy silence was a group of about ten women who were talking and smiling and seemed to be having a great time.

The gate opened, and the guards let everyone through without checking people. As the large wagon of wool moved onto the street, one of its back wheels broke on the first cobblestone and scattered the wool everywhere.

One of the ladies in the loud group exclaimed, "I hope that doesn't slow down the looms today. I am going to crush my record!"

The rest of the women laughed but moved out of the way. An old farmer was looking at the wagon wheel, trying to figure out what he was going to do, as the guards came over to see about the holdup. The wagon had broken down and was straddling the threshold of the gate, keeping it from being able to close.

The guard in red said, "We need your wagon moved quickly because it's blocking the way for everyone, and if we needed to close the gate suddenly, we wouldn't be able to. How long will it take you to fix it?"

"Don't know," the farmer tersely replied. "Thought it was fine this morning when I checked over everything. The best course is to unload it, move the wagon, and then fix it. Problem is, I'm the only one here to unload. The factory was going to help me unload when I got there, but they're not going to be able to have anyone here for at least an hour."

As the kids walked over to the down cart, Warren saw a cat that looked just like Honor running down the street. He cried out about her being in the town and took off down the road. Penelope and Gretchen started to run after Warren but then gave up.

"Pen, just let him go. We have things to do," Gretchen said as she slowed down to a walk.

Sinclair approached the farmer. "I'm new in town, but if you want, I can give you a hand."

"That's mighty kind of you, young man," he replied, shaking Sinclair's hand. "We need to unload all the wool to the street and then get the wagon moved before I can even see what needs to happen to fix it."

The two started to work on unloading each bale of wool together, as neither of them could move one by himself.

***

The girls followed the group of loud ladies to the factory. They knew from what their parents had told them that factories tended to always need people, so they were hopeful that they might get some work. The building looked like a huge barn. The first few feet of its walls were made of stone, and then they turned into clapboard. In the middle of the building were large open barn doors, and off to one side was a normal house door. Horses brought wagons in and out of the factory, and pulleys moved various bundles all over the place.

The girls walked up to the normal door and found a two-foot-tall gnome behind a counter. It was hard to tell exactly how old he was, but based on his facial features, he was probably no older than Gretchen. He had glasses perched on his long wiggly nose, and his purple-and-pink eyes watched them as they walked up.

"We're looking for work and would like to know if there's anything we could do," Penelope said.

The gnome flashed a toothy smile, hopped down from his stool, and headed through the door. "We always need more in the weaving room. If you follow me, I'll introduce you to the foreman."

As they traveled through the factory, they saw a section for each task. It started with people spinning wool into yarn and progressed to large vats for dying and huge looms where weavers were working in teams to make big projects. There was even a team running around, preparing the factory for the day's work. Baskets were being carried, and carts were pushed between and around people. It was a huge mess of energy and motion, with people and hand-cranked machines all moving and making noise. For Gretchen, it was more noise than she'd ever heard and more people than she liked to be around at one time.

"Girls, let me introduce you to the weaving foreman." The gnome pointed to a man in nicer clothing. Then he turned and went back the way he'd come, ducking and dodging.

"Ahh, two new workers! I can get you right to work today. Were you told how we pay?" the foreman asked.

"No, we weren't," Penelope replied.

"Well, we pay by the frame," the foreman cheerfully boomed. "Each one you do, we grade on quality. The better the quality, the more you get paid, and the more looms you finish, the more you get paid as well!" He clapped his hands and smiled at the girls. "Now, if you follow me, I can take you to the lady who makes the best cloth we offer so that you can see how she works and learn what to do from her!"

He turned and took them back into the moving chaos of the factory. They soon

found themselves near a corner. A lady who looked to be in her late twenties was standing at a loom that was two arm's lengths in each direction and as tall as she was. Behind her was a table where tools were neatly arranged. In the mess of the building, her area was neat and tidy. It also was quieter than elsewhere, as the bales of wool were stacked in the walkway next to her.

"Elle, I want you to show these two ladies how to use our looms and how to make the best wool that they can. I'll be back in an hour to take them away, so please make sure they're ready." The man turned and walked off.

"Well, as you know, I'm Elle. I'm going to show you what I do to make the best cloth in this building. Every day, I turn in the highest-quality fabric. Part of what goes into making the best is using the right yarn." She walked over to the table of tools. "Some are better than others, and sometimes, you need to fix the yarn."

Elle spent the next fifteen minutes teaching the girls what each tool was called and how to use them in different ways. She then showed them how to pick the best yarn and how to smooth it out to make it look just right. After that, she demonstrated how to put it on the loom. She took the rest of the time showing the girls how to weave the yarn and comb it into place. Elle gave careful instructions for each step, which Penelope furiously wrote down in her notebook.

"Now, girls, this is how you put the warp onto the shed stick and how you use the leash rod and the heddle rod," Elle said.

While Penelope tried to pay attention to each detail and asked questions, somewhere between "how to make the weft" and "how to weave the whole loom," Gretchen decided it was possible to climb from one ceiling rafter to the next if you had a tall-enough ladder to start with, which must have been how they opened the windows that high up. The time went by quickly, and although Gretchen was mostly confused, Penelope's notebook had just enough information to get them started.

At the end of the hour, the foreman gathered the girls and showed them their looms. Gretchen needed a smaller loom since she couldn't reach high enough to use a full one.

"Now, little lady, since you're using a halfling's loom, which is about half the size of the full loom, you need to finish two for every one that someone does on the full loom for your pay to be the same," the foreman said and walked away.

Chapter Eleven

"Your dad is the hardest worker I know, and I love that about him. In fact, I'm not sure if I love his work ethic, or his muscles more, they go together."

—Mary Bishop to Sinclair

Sinclair wiped the sweat off his brow as he leaned against a wall. He had just helped the farmer and the other workers unload the last bit of wool from the cart in the factory loading area and was ready for a break. The farmer took a lot fewer breaks than Sinclair was used to, but since he and his siblings really needed the money and he didn't want to seem lazy, he'd pushed himself hard to keep up the pace.

"Well, that was a good bit of work this morning that I hadn't planned on. Thank you for your help with fixing the wagon. I have more work back at the farm if you want it," the farmer said.

"I would love more work. Like I said, we're passing through and low on supplies, so any chance to help is appreciated."

The two men rode from the weaving factory back out of town. What should have been an hour-long trip for the farmer had taken more than four since he'd needed to unload, repair, and reload his wagon. They took the same road out of town that the kids had walked in on and passed the large wagon. The farmer looked at it but said nothing. Soon, they arrived at a farm with fields for grazing. They were both tired, but as they pulled up, another man came out to greet them with a bounce in his step and a smile on his face.

The farmer jumped down from the buckboard. "Harry, take the wagon around for us, please, and then meet me back near the garden. We had a breakdown, and this young man stepped in to help, so I offered him some more work. I was thinking you could show him where the fence posts should go."

"That works, boss," Harry said and took the wagon around.

The farmer walked off and waved for Sinclair to follow. "Sinclair, right over here is my garden. I'm needing to add new fence posts around it since the old ones broke down. Does that sound like something that you can do?"

"Digging is something that I can do," Sinclair said happily. "I know we didn't talk about pay before with the wagon, but how much are you paying for the posts?

"I figure that you can get paid two coppers per post that you dig and sink correctly."

"I got the wagon dropped, and the ox is in its stall, so I can show him where to dig the holes," Harry said on his way over from the barn.

The farmer left, and Harry showed Sinclair where the tools and the posts were. They already had thirty posts ready to be planted and would have the last ten in the next couple of days. Harry marked out each spot where they wanted a post.

"Just checking with you before I head over for my work. You know how to dig a posthole, right?" Harry asked.

Sinclair, a little offended that he would even be asked, rolled his eyes. "Of course I do." Then he mumbled under his breath, "How hard can digging a few holes be?" He huffed and went to grab a shovel from the shed.

The rest of the day, Sinclair dug holes with the shovel, pulling out rocks of all sizes. To get deep enough to make a post stand up, Sinclair had to dig rather large holes. Then he would drop the post in and try to pack it with the rocks he'd found. After a long, hard day, Sinclair had put in fifteen posts.

As the day wound down, the farmer and Harry came back over. They walked by and pushed on the posts. Most of them fell over, but two of the fifteen were still standing. The farmer looked sad, and Harry was just shaking his head.

"Well, son, it looks like you got two good posts in. So that's four coppers, and I'll throw in another six from what you did with the wagon today. So I owe you ten coppers."

The farmer pulled out his money bag and handed him the coins. Sinclair looked down the line of posts that had been pushed over. The two still standing had the most rocks in them, so he thought he might be able to fix everything the next day.

“Can I come back tomorrow and fix the other ones and get paid?” Sinclair asked.

“Would work out real well if you did, and I can even feed you lunch tomorrow,” the farmer replied.

They shook hands, and Sinclair started back toward his wagon. Shadowing behind him as he walked, just out of his line of sight, was a large smoky-gray-and-copper cat silently padding along. If he had seen her, he would have known that this cat had a disappointed expression on her very majestic face.

***

Warren was waiting in the wagon when his sisters got back. As they came in, he showed them the water he'd drawn from the town well and the nuts he'd found. He'd busied himself, trying to gather things they could use and he was big enough to carry. The children were looking at the little bit they'd acquired when Sinclair came in and dropped into a chair, dirty and tired.

“That was a long day. I did great at my job and got paid ten coppers for the day's work. We should see what we can buy for dinner.” Sinclair drank down a mug of water and filled a second one.

"Ugh, Slair. Go wash up. You're dirty, and you stink," Penelope said.

Sinclair went out and washed off his arms and face, using the buckets on the outside of the old wagon. There was nothing to dry off with, so he dried his hands on his dirty pants and went back inside.

"Like I was saying, I did great today, so let's go find some food," Sinclair said as they left the wagon.

The Bishop children headed back into the market, where Sinclair was shocked to find that after he bought each of them a meat pie and a loaf of bread and picked up a sewing kit to fix his torn pants, the money was gone. Penelope tried to talk him into buying cheaper food and something for himself as a gift.

"Sorry, Pen. I'm fine. It's amazing how fast money goes when you're on your own. Plus, it's different when you earned the money people are using to give you gifts."

They took everything back to the wagon to eat. Sinclair was kind of bummed about his birthday, but he was providing for his sisters and brother, and that gave him a sense of maturity, which was a nice feeling. Besides, all he had to do the next day was make the holes he'd already dug deeper and fill them with more rocks, and he would make as much money as he had that day.

"So, how did your day go, Pen?" Sinclair asked as he finished off his dinner.

"It went well. Gretchen and I learned how to weave from the best lady in the factory. While we were both slow, I'm sure tomorrow we'll speed up enough that we can get paid for a loom of work," Penelope said with a strained smile.

"So you didn't get paid?" Sinclair asked with a start.

Penelope gave a big sigh. "No. We had a late start having to learn the job, and then it was slow work. I'm sure that we'll finish the minimum for payment tomorrow."

Sinclair was about to say something else when there was a scratching at the door. Warren jumped up and opened it, and Honor hopped into the room. She walked daintily across the room and jumped into Gretchen's lap. The huge cat sniffed at the last bite of the meat pie and turned a full circle before she lay down with her head on one of Gretchen's knees and started to purr.

"There you are!" Warren said, shaking his head and grinning. "I've been looking for you all day after I saw you run past the broken wagon." He looked at his siblings with a smile plastered on his face and his eyes wide open. "I saw her at the broken wagon, and then I chased her across half the town before I caught her. I brought her back, put her in the wagon, and then went to get water. When I came back, she was gone. I looked all over for a way that she could get out, and I just couldn't find one."

He took a huge breath and bounced up and down on his toes and then blurted, "I found a whole shelf of Grandpa Alexander's journals. I looked at them for a bit, and they seem to be about the business deals he had while he was on this wagon. I also found a map that looks like it's a route the wagon takes."

Warren ran over to the drawers, pulled out a leather map, and unfolded it on the table. Then he pointed to the different dots and shapes. "See, here on the left-hand side is this list of numbers. The number fifteen is next to Cnoc, and here's Collina, listed next to the number one. I think that we must have made a circle and went from fifteen to one on the list, which means the next place the wagon will go is Deal. It's not that far away."

The other three children gathered around the map. Cnoc was on the top right side. On the bottom left was the number one for Collina. There were mountains and rivers between the Bishops and their home. Based on the map, it was a huge distance to cover. Walking home could take them years. The children sat, absorbed in their thoughts.

"Well, this seems to tell us where we are," Sinclair softly said.

"Yeah. I'm thinking we're not walking home from here, so it's going to be more of a long ride back in the wagon," Pen said a little too calmly.

Gretchen was crying and started to pet Honor, who had stayed on her lap. "How long do you fink it will take?" she asked between sobs.

"No idea, but maybe those journals will give some insight as to how long this trip will be," Sinclair said.

Pen sat up straight and pulled out her paper. "Right. So, let's make a list of the things we need to do to get home. The first, I guess, is to get Slair his class so we have more to work with. Then we need to figure out everything else."

"Right, my class..." Sinclair had spent most of the day working hard and tried not to feel sorry for himself and the fact his birthday had gone sideways. "I checked while I was at the farm today, and I have three options. I can choose to be a beggar, a store clerk, or a farmhand."

"Wow, that doesn't sound like we have much to work with. Can you read to us what each one says it does?" Penelope asked.

"Yeah. Let me open my book... 'Beggar: You gain the active class skill of Induce Pity and the passive skill of Reduce Food Consumption. You have access to this because someone has taken pity on you and given you more money than you should have gotten. Store clerk: You gain the active skill of Defuse Anger and the passive skill of Better Deals. You have access to this class because your parents have suffered countless hours and sleepless nights teaching you a set of marketable skills. Farmhand: You gain two passive skills, Increased Stamina and Sun Resistance. You have access to this class because you somehow got hired on as a farmhand.'"

The oldest Bishop scrunched his brow, blew out a deep breath, and muttered, "That's odd."

"What?" asked Gretchen.

"I have a fourth option that just showed up. It's marked *rare* and *developing* and is called Tolerable Trekking Trader. It has the active skills of Hawking Goods and Negotiation, with a passive skill of Full Access, but there's an asterisk beside it, and I can't figure out what that means."

"Does it say why you have access to that terrible tracking trader?" Warren asked.

"No, and it's tolerable trekking trader," Sinclair said.

Penelope spoke up. "I think you should hold off on taking any class until we can figure out what some of the things mean. It just makes sense, considering what Dad said. We already know what advantages store clerks get with their class, from the ones who worked with Dad, but putting in some research makes sense."

"Yeah, that sounds like a good idea. I think I'm going to read some of those journals and see if Grandpa has this class too. It would be good to get an idea of what to expect." Sinclair grabbed one of the journals and went outside, where it was still light.

Penelope, following suit, took one of the other journals and went out. Soon, Gretchen dumped Honor off her lap and grabbed another book and went out too. Smiling, Warren picked up Honor and put her on her pillow, almost dropping her twice. Then he grabbed a book and took it outside as well.

Chapter Twelve

"A man with a class ability that lets him swim, will outswim a fish."

—A common proverb

Yesterday went horribly wrong for us as a family. We didn't make much money, so we only had enough for dinner. We need to do better at our jobs today and make more." Penelope pulled apart their last small loaf of bread and passed it around. "This is what we have for the day, so please, let's each do our part."

"I'm going to work even harder today. Digging posts isn't easy, but I can go faster for the first half of the day today and then check everything and fix any problems. I'm sure I'll make enough money for food today and some for tomorrow too." Sinclair gave a big smile.

Gretchen looked thoughtful. "I'm not going back to *th*e weaving factory. I didn't get money from it because my arms are too short to work the loom, and *th*e other jobs they *th*ought I could do didn't pay much." She frowned at her older siblings. "I'm just too small for most *th*ings in the factory. I'm going to see if I can find work in a shop like I did for our parents."

The kids ate their bread and drank the water they'd pulled from the town well the day before. It wasn't much, but they added in some of the berries they had left, along with the last of the nuts. Warren tried to get into a nut, but it wouldn't crack for him, so he started to hit it and yell.

Sinclair shouted, "Stop it, Ren! That's not how you crack a nut!"

Warren threw it at Sinclair. "Who made you boss? You're not Dad!"

Sinclair stood up and towered over Warren. "I'm the oldest, and our parents always say that I'm in charge when they leave, and they're not here, so I'm in charge—and yesterday, Penelope even said I was in charge! Now, calm down and don't throw things at me, and I'll show you how I crack a nut!"

Warren backed away with a grin on his face that could only mean trouble. "Well, I would be with our parents if I hadn't listened to you and gone into the barn, so maybe they were wrong to put you in charge!" He grabbed the door, threw it open, and ran toward the woods.

Sinclair was taking a few steps to follow when Gretchen said, "Slair, let him go. You have to get to *th*e farm, and he'll be back. He's just hungry. You know how he gets when he needs to eat."

"Yeah, and he misses home like we all do," Penelope chimed in. "It's not your fault we're here. We all made the choice to follow. We all chose to get off task, and now none of us are at home. Also, I'm not sure I put you in charge. It's more that Dad always says you are."

Sinclair took a few deep breaths, rubbing his forehead where the nut had hit him. "I shouldn't have snapped like that at him. Things will be better tonight when we have more food. Pen, you're going back to weave today, right?"

"Yup. I know what I did wrong yesterday. I didn't take enough time setting everything up, so the quality of my work was too low to get top pay. If I do everything perfectly, then I should make lots of money. It's easy work. I just need to focus on what I'm doing and do it completely right," Pen said with a determined expression on her face.

***

Warren had run for about ten minutes before he slowed down. After the first turn, he knew that his brother wasn't following him, but he liked to run. The woods were a fun place to be and full of good things. The day before, he'd found a bush covered in berries and had eaten all of them himself. He was sure that if he put his mind to it, he could catch a squirrel or rabbit for dinner. It wouldn't be much, he knew, but maybe it would show his brother that he could be useful.

Warren wandered around the woods for the better part of the morning. As he went, he filled his pockets with little things he thought could be useful. He picked up some shiny rocks and found a nice stick that he sharpened into a spearpoint. He was planning to use it to hunt. Of course, he really didn't have any experience hunting, so that worked about as well as you could expect. With his left hand, he tossed rocks into bushes to try to scare things out of them and then threw his spear at whatever came out. He missed so completely that the animals didn't even know anything had been thrown.

As the sun rose high in the sky, Warren heard something big moving through the woods. He turned with his spear held high and was ready to throw when a tall man with a big, full beard came through the bushes. He had a jolly smile and held, over his shoulder, a long pole with several small dead animals.

"Whoa there! Don't throw that spear! I'm friendly!" the man called.

"Oh! I thought you were a bear or a monster." Warren sighed as he lowered his little spear.

"Well, I've been called both, but I'm neither," the man said with genuine good cheer. "So, if you don't mind my asking, what is a young man like you doing out this far in the woods?"

"I'm hunting, like you!"

"I'm trapping, not hunting—far easier while perhaps more time-consuming," the man said.

Surprised, Warren asked, "Trapping?"

"Yup. I've trapped in these woods for years. I have several traps that I move around, and each day, I get enough meat for myself and some to sell. It's nothing big, but it works in the background while I am doing my other work."

"Can you teach me?" Warren asked excitedly.

"There's really nothing much to it. I can show you how to set up some simple snares, but most of it is knowing where to put the traps and then waiting for them to work." The man dropped his catch to the ground. "Once I show you how to make a snare, you'll want to practice making it so that you can set it up right the first time. The more you mess with traps, the more they smell like you and the less likely they are to work, so doing it right from the start is better than making little corrections the whole time. Set it right and then leave it alone to work."

"So, is there anything dangerous around in these woods I should know about?" Warren asked, thinking back to the boar.

"No. With all the shepherds, there's nothing much dangerous around anymore."

"That's good to hear. I wouldn't want to get chased around by something here."

The big man chuckled and got to work showing Warren how to make a snare out of twigs, bark, and vines. He demonstrated how to bend back a small tree to make a spring for the trap. "If you get a big enough tree and snare, you can even snag a larger animal. Not many of those around here, but you can always give it a try." He grinned.

The two spent several hours making snares and springs. Warren learned how to use a small knife to strip bark to make cord and how to spot rabbit trails. Then the man headed off to his home and his other work.

CHAPTER THIRTEEN

"When you're in business with someone, never lie. It doesn't help—it breaks the trust you need to build, and forgiveness gets harder when money is involved. Own your mistakes, and your business partner, if they're good, will help you grow."

—Charles Bishop

Gretchen had spent all morning looking for work that a twelve-year-old could do. Though she knew a lot about working in her parents' store, it was kind of hard to get a temporary job in a shop. Her chores at home were things like stocking the shelves and cleaning up the storefront. She also helped her mother balance the store ledger since it was just simple arithmetic. While her dad had taken the merchant class and knew what he was doing, her mom loved the details of doing math and making all the numbers zero out.

Gretchen was getting kind of down on herself when she came into the hatter's store. As she looked around, she was amazed. The room was lit from huge glass windows in the front that were no doubt enchanted. The shelves were lined with beautiful hats of all types, and Gretchen was impressed by the variety and craftsmanship of each piece. There were tall men's hats and some of the most intricate bonnets that she'd ever seen. There were ribbons and feathers and colors everywhere.

As she walked up to the front counter to see if there was any work available, she heard little kids happily yelling from the door leading to the part of the store that was the family's home. She could hear a baby fussing and two other voices that sounded like kids younger than Ren. They were playing. She rang the little bell to let people know she was at the counter.

"Dear, my hands are a mess. I'm felting right now. Can you check the counter?" a man yelled from behind another door.

"Coming!" a woman's pleasant but tired voice called from the living section.

A kind, exhausted-looking lady came in from the back, holding a young baby on her hip. She wore a nice lavender dress with ribbon running through the skirt and had a matching bonnet. It was clear that the baby was so tired she couldn't take a nap because she fussed and rubbed her eyes instead of laying her head on her mom's shoulder.

"Hello. Welcome to Higgins Hats and Bonnets. How can I help you today?" the lady asked.

"Hi. I'm Gretchen. I'm from out of town and will be here for a little while. I wanted to see if you might ha*ve* any work for me. My parents ha*ve* a store where we're from, so I know how to do *th*ings around a store, and I have a kid bro*th*er, so I know how to help wi*th* kids too." Gretchen gave her best store smile and prayed that the lady understood her. Her parents had taught her how to be polite and helpful to potential customers, but most of the time, she tried not to talk unless it was absolutely necessary. Things were a lot better now than when she was younger because she had worked very hard to learn to speak, but she still had to think about how to say words and remembered the confused looks people would give her mom. There were even a couple of years, when she was four or five, when she just meowed at people instead of talking, which probably added to the confusion. Thankfully, most people were at least polite, although she got used to other kids asking her why she talked funny.

"Good to meet you, Gretchen. I would shake your hand, but mine are full. I'm Mrs. Higgins. I'm not sure I have any work for you in our shop right now. Mr. Higgins is working on hats, so I don't want to disturb him..."

The baby started fussing again just as a couple walked through the door. Mrs. Higgins looked from the baby to Gretchen and back to the couple, who were obviously well-off. She passed the baby to Gretchen. "Please take Ruby to the back. Jake and Harold are both down for their naps right now. I'll be back in just a few minutes after I take care of the needs of our esteemed customers, the governor and his wife."

Gretchen took Ruby and bounced her and patted her back as she walked to the back of the store. She could hear Mrs. Higgins talking with the customers in front but couldn't make out much of what was said. Gretchen carried the baby over to a rocking chair, set her down, and started to rock.

Around twenty minutes later, Mrs. Higgins came back in to find Ruby passed out on Gretchen's shoulder. "Thank you so much! She's normally asleep at this time of day, so I'm able to take care of customers while my husband is felting," Mrs. Higgins said with a smile. "It looks like you're good with kids. Could I get you to sit with her for a while longer while I do some work?"

"Sure. I love babies. Your two boys seem to still be in *th*eir room, so I'm guessing *th*ey're asleep since I never *s*aw *th*em."

Mrs. Higgins gave Gretchen a thankful smile, heaved a sigh of frustration, and got to work. On one end of the table, Mrs. Higgins placed a very large ledger and a basket of loose papers along with a quill, blotter, and inkwell. She opened the ledger and pulled out a blank sheet.

Gretchen sighed, relieved. *Things are going to work out. She understood me and is thankful for my help. It's probably because she has little kids and is used to listening to them…*

Gretchen's thoughts were interrupted by a loud sigh. Mrs. Higgins was counting on her fingers and scratching out the math on the empty page. She got more upset as she was working. She murmured a few times and then tried again, counting and making tallies on the spare page.

"Ugh, this just isn't adding up!" The lady stood up and stretched. She looked over at Gretchen. "You said you worked in your parents' store. Did you ever help with the math for the ledger?"

"Ye*s*, my mom and I used to do it every week in the *sl*ow times and daily during the busy *s*eason." Gretchen spoke softly so as not to wake Ruby up.

"Why don't you pass me Ruby. I'll lay her down on the bed, and you take a look at my numbers and see if you can figure out why they're not adding up."

Mrs. Higgins got up and took the baby, and Gretchen walked over to look at the ledger. There were six columns per page, each titled across the top. They were ordered left to right: *Name*, *Description*, *Date*, *Debit*, *Credit*, and *Balance*. The first column contained names of the people who'd bought something or whom money had been given to. The second column contained descriptions of what had been sold or bought—just a few words to remind the person reading what was going on. The *Debit* column recorded any money that came into the business, and the *Credit* column was for anytime money went out. Her mom had explained that even though some people thought that credits were to add money and debits were to take money away, it was actually backward because accounting was done from the perspective of the business. Each change of the debit or credit would be added or subtracted from the balance line above it. That way, the business owners would know how much money they had.

If the books were kept right, a person could follow the math all the way back to when the business first began, with the beginning balance of seed money. This ledger had lots of adding and subtracting, and it was not as straightforward as it could have been. It took a while for Gretchen to figure out what she was looking at. The hat store's books were different from her parents' books because the money was marked in total values and not the lowest values. Gretchen's parents had taught her to reduce the ledger to coppers, so *75g 15s 89c* in the hat store ledger would have been *751589c* in her parents' book. Each gold piece was worth one hundred silvers, and each silver piece was worth one hundred coppers. Gretchen's parents also did double-entry accounting, which was much more complicated but better for them because of the types of things they sold and did.

Gretchen scrunched up her nose and studied the book in front of her. She wasn't sure what the problem was, but the lady seemed to think there was one. "So, before I start trying to find *th*e problem in the ledger, what makes you *th*ink *th*ere's an error?" she asked as Mrs. Higgins came back in.

"Well, we have one gold and twelve silvers too much in the box, and I've already asked my husband, and no one has tipped us. That means something is wrong in the math. Here are the copies of our sales receipts for the past month. It all added up correctly last month." Mrs. Higgins pointed to the basket.

Gretchen went through each receipt, put them in order of date, and then started the process of matching each piece of paper to the ledger. Mrs. Higgins helped her by calling out the numbers as they went through. After thirty minutes, they found the mistake. It had happened when the store had bought something and marked down that they'd spent gold when in fact they'd spent silver. This caused the whole math problem to trickle down from the tenth day of the month.

The lady smiled and hugged Gretchen. "Thank you. I never would have thought to check the math the way you did. What made you change everything to coppers on the page before you got started?"

"My mom and dad make us keep it all in coppers. They said that doing it that way shows problems faster. You were looking for a gold problem when you had a silver problem, and that was why you couldn't find it. I was looking for a total problem and was able to find it that way." Gretchen gave a happy smile.

"Well, I'm glad we got that taken care of," Mrs. Higgins said with a big smile. "I didn't want to have to go down to the banker and have them look over my books again just because I had too much money. I don't trust that he would have found the money as much as saying that someone overpaid to balance out my books. I would have had to pay him too. Speaking of which, how much do I owe you?"

A huge lump gathered in Gretchen's throat. They hadn't discussed anything beforehand, but she'd never been paid real money for helping her parents. The Higgins had several kids to feed. Gretchen had also just seen how much money they had in their business account, and she didn't want to be seen as greedy or selfish.

"Could I get a bonnet like yours?" Gretchen asked sheepishly.

"Oh, that would be lovely. I have just the one for you." Mrs. Higgins got up from the table. "We can mark this one as sold for services. It's a bit small for most of the people around here because we made it as a mock-up for the one we're selling to the governor's wife. I think that the dark green will complement your brown eyes nicely."

A few moments later, she came back in with a nice light-blue bonnet decorated with a dark-green ribbon. The ribbon was woven through the front of the bonnet in such a way as to be seen and accent the blue. A thinner green ribbon was used in the back to make adjustments for where Gretchen's hair would go. Across the top of the bonnet was a thin cutout-lace design.

Gretchen's eyes grew big. "Oh! Dat's so pretty!" she squealed.

CHAPTER FOURTEEN

"There is no such thing as failure, only things that work or lessons about what doesn't. So don't be afraid to take risks, unless you're in a dungeon.
In fact, just stay out of dungeons entirely! They're where people with no regard for their own safety go to get rich fast."

—Mary Bishop - Two Sisters 1139

When the kids got back together after the workday, they agreed to talk about how much they'd earned and what they'd done. None of them seemed super excited. Warren was the first to go, as he was always the happy one. He opened his eyes wide and plastered a smile on his face that showed his teeth and threatened to swallow his whole head if it was any bigger.

"Today, I learned all about making traps! I met this trapper out in the woods, and he was collecting animals from traps he'd set the day before. He was as big as a bear, and I almost threw my spear at him. He was super nice, and when I told him I was hunting squirrels, he laughed and showed me how to make traps. It was hard, but I think I can make one, and then he showed me a good place to leave it. He said if I don't mess with it, my scent will go away, and I'll catch something."

"So you spent all day playing in the woods while we tried to get coin to buy food," Sinclair scoffed. "Mom and Dad aren't here to take care of us anymore, so we all have to pull our weight. You can't just run around playing like you used to do. Stop trying to make up stories about your grand adventures. Get back to real life."

Gretchen muttered, "I believe him. I saw a guy today *th*at looked like a bear and had lots of game on a stick."

"Well, even if that guy was real, that doesn't mean that he taught Ren anything. I mean, where's his catch?" Sinclair said, leaning back and crossing his arms.

"I did too learn! I'll bring something tomorrow—I'm sure of it!" Ren yelled.

"Now, Ren, don't go and steal. We might not be as well-off as we used to be, but that doesn't mean we should take from others. Just find something to do in town, like sweeping, and you can help pay for dinner." Penelope patted Warren's head like he was a dog.

Warren ducked out from under Penelope and walked over to Honor. He unceremoniously picked up the cat. "You believe me, right, girl?"

Purring, Honor stood up from her pillow, put her front paws on Warren's chest, and headbutted his chin, softly pushing on him. Then he picked her up and moved near his bed and sat down with her on his lap. He turned his shoulder to the rest of them and just looked at Honor and hugged her.

"Well, today I found work doing math!" Gretchen said with a small smile. "I first thought that I was getting hired to watch the hatter's baby, but then I ended up helping them get their store ledger to balance. It was fun working on a ledger. It reminded me of Mom since we used to do the books at home."

Penelope's eyes lit up. She knew working on people's books could mean good money. "How much did you get paid?"

Gretchen pulled out her bonnet and put it on with a smile. "Well, that's a kind of odd story. We didn't talk about pay before I started to work because the governor and his wife came in, and I had to take Mrs. Higgins's baby to the back. Then we just kind of kept working, and at the end of the day, this lovely bonnet is what I got."

"What? We need money for food, and you worked for a bonnet? Maybe you can sell it and we can get food," Sinclair said, looking angrily at Gretchen.

"Well, it's not like I asked for it," Gretchen lied, looking at the ground. "But it truly is nice, and it fits me. I'm not sure anyone else would want it, but I guess I could try to sell it tomorrow."

Penelope sighed. "I guess it's my turn. I did much better today. Well, the quality of my work, I'm sure, was better. I took my time and made sure that everything I did was perfect and even checked each thread twice before moving on. The problem was, I didn't finish enough today to get paid. I'm sure I'll finish the segment tomorrow, and then I can get paid for it. I'm just not sure how others get so much done. They said that it's a good-paying job as long as you can do the task. It seems easy, but there are so many steps, and each one is so long."

Gretchen looked at Sinclair, who hadn't said much. "Slair, how was your job on *th*e farm today?"

Sinclair lowered his shoulders. "I almost got fired today."

Gretchen gasped. "Why? What happened?"

"I thought I needed to work harder and faster. So I pushed hard the first half of the day and managed to do as much as I did yesterday, but the problem was, the posts didn't stand up at all. The farmer was mad that not only had I spent all day making bad holes, but I—and I quote—'did a worse job today than yesterday.' If the old farmhand hadn't gotten him to give me another chance, I would be looking for a job tomorrow. On the other hand, Harry said he would show me what to do tomorrow to make it all work. I'm hoping that I can get paid then. I only got three coppers today, which is enough for a loaf of bread."

Warren, sitting on the ground with his back to his brother, laughed and mockingly said, "What, you can't dig a hole in the ground well enough to get paid? Like you said, Mom and Dad aren't here to take care of us. You can't just play in the dirt all day. We need food!"

"Shut up, you little worm!" yelled Sinclair as Ren stood up.

"You two, stop!" both girls said, standing up and keeping Sinclair from punching his grinning brother again.

***

Honor walked around and through everyone's legs. If the kids had been paying attention, they would have seen a tired and exasperated expression on her face. She questioned the wisdom of taking all four children with her in the first place but ultimately decided that they were overall decent humans and would figure things out. None of the kids noticed her expression, but they did get distracted from their fight when she jumped up on the table and knocked the mugs of water onto the leather map.

Chapter Fifteen

"The fact that the kingdom could get both dwarves and gnomes to work on the same projects was a testament to the rulers of the time."

—A History of the Lost Kingdom: Jonathan Counting - Two Sisters 1053

The next morning, Warren was first up. He tended to fall to sleep faster than everyone else, and the bunks were not very comfortable with just boards and a little hay. So he woke up as the sun rose and went out with their one pot to get water. It would have been nice if there were some oats they could heat up, but they only had the nuts they'd found in the woods on the first day, a few wild onions, and a bit of bread.

When Warren got back, he saw Honor, who he'd made sure to not let out, sitting next to the door with a fresh rabbit at her feet. She gave him an amused look and then pawed at the door, breaking off some of the chipped paint. He opened the door for her, trying to figure out how the cat had gotten out yet again. He'd spent most of the first day climbing in and around the wagon, looking for ways to get in and out other than the windows and doors.

When his siblings got up, he had the rabbit skinned and a fire going in the beat-up stove. In fact, they woke up because he'd forgotten about the vent pipe, and the smoke had filled the wagon until he was able to get the pipe open. Penelope took over from him, making rabbit soup, and they opened the windows and door, which cleared the smoke out.

"Where did the rabbit come from?" Sinclair asked.

"I was bringing back water, and Honor was sitting at the door with it, and then she just was pawing to get in. I was only out long enough to go down to the river and back. I made sure she was in the wagon when I left, so I don't know how she got out, but she did." Ren looked confusedly at the sleeping cat.

"So not from one of your traps, then?" Sinclair asked, laughing and rolling his eyes.

"No, Slair. I haven't gone to look at the traps, so it's not from one of them," Warren responded dryly. Then he grinned. "But I will tonight, and we'll have lots of meat!"

"Food's ready!" Penelope turned toward the cat, gave a soft smile, and said, "Thank you for the rabbit."

As the kids started to eat, they talked a bit about what they would be doing that day.

"I'm going to go back to see if I can get any more work with Mrs. Higgins," Gretchen said.

"Try to get paid in money today," Sinclair said, laughing.

Gretchen smiled as she ate her soup. "Okay, I'll see what happens."

"I'm going to finish my section of fabric today. I'm sure if I have enough focus and follow my list of things to do, I can get the best section out," Penelope said with no small amount of pride. "Perhaps if you put as much effort into doing things right, as I do, then your job on the farm would work out today." She pointed her spoon at Sinclair.

"I'm going to be working hard today. That's what matters with work on a farm—doing the tough things. It's not all about being perfect but about digging right. Harry is going to show me what to do, so I should be able to learn how to get the posts to stay up better." Sinclair sighed. "Just don't know what I'm doing wrong."

"Ren, make sure you ask around to see if you can sweep out a store or something. No more playing in the woods. We need food, and you're not going to get that just by playing around all day," Penelope said as she cleared off the table.

Each of the children left the wagon. Sinclair went directly to the farm to dig more postholes. Penelope and Gretchen headed into town, Pen to work at the weaving factory and her sister to see if the hatter needed more help. As the girls were leaving, Penelope called for Ren to walk with them, probably assuming he would look for work in town. Before long, though, she had to turn off the road to go to the factory, and Gretchen departed as well. Warren turned right back around and ran for the forest to check on his traps.

***

Sinclair got to the farm in time to start the day of work. As he walked up, he saw the farmer pointing to where he'd messed up digging the day before, and his hopeful feelings for the new day went right out the window. He got close enough to hear.

"This is his last chance," the farmer said. "He doesn't listen much to me at all and thinks he knows what's best and then does things halfway. He has dug these holes twice, and we don't have room for error now. If we loosen too much of the dirt, we'll have to shift the whole fence."

"I'll show him what needs to happen. Some people need a little bit more hands-on guidance. I sure did when I was that age," Harry said.

At that point, the farmer saw Sinclair. "Son, you have one try left to do what needs to be done, with no goofing off, or you'll have to find another job around here, and not many people will hire someone who doesn't do good work for me," he said gruffly.

Sinclair looked at the ground, feeling scared. "I can do a good job today."

"You'd better. Harry, he's all yours." The farmer walked off toward the other end of the property.

"Okay, Sinclair, we have our work cut out for ourselves today." Harry grabbed Sinclair's shoulder. "I know that you can dig fast, but you've been digging all wrong. Once a hole is dug, it takes over a year before the ground settles enough for another try in that spot. So we're going to have to be careful because we need to make sure we're doing it right the first time." He pointed to the tool shed. "Grab the narrow shovel, not the big one that you've been using. Once we get the holes going, then I'll show you how to split the posts. We might as well teach you how to do the whole job, from start to finish, the right way."

Sinclair went to the shed and got the narrow shovel. When he returned, Harry had already started to move off. Over one shoulder, he had a huge hammer, and in his other hand, he was carrying a couple of wedges. Sinclair had to run to catch up to him, but they arrived at the first posthole at about the same time.

"Hand me the shovel and take a look at what I'm doing. I'm going to talk to you like you're an adult today, and you can either learn or find a new job." Harry took the shovel from Sinclair and started to dig straight down, not at the low, easy angle Sinclair had been using. He would place the shovel and then slam his foot down on the back edge then pry back the handle just a little. He then placed the shovel so that half of the blade was overlapping part of the cut that was already in the ground and repeated the process until he'd cut a four-inch-across circle the depth of the shovel.

"Now, once you get all the way around like this, you can try to pull the whole plug out, or you can cut it in half. Most people try to pull the whole thing out, but that doesn't tend to work because the bottom is still connected. So I cut it in half, starting in the middle of the plug and aiming toward the side away from me."

Harry placed the shovel again and stomped on the lip and then pulled back hard. Then he dropped the shovel to the side,

reached down, and grabbed the plug. He pulled half of it out and then moved to the other one.

"Now, that's the easy part!" Harry said with a half smile that spoke of hard work and bad jokes. "Next, we have to go another whole length in the hole, but to do so is going to be hard. You've been avoiding using the right tool the past two days, so now we have no margin for error." He picked up a long, heavy metal bar with a small wedge on the top. "This is a digging pole. It's how we can go deep enough to drop a post in. Once you get down there and pull the loose dirt, we'll use this to make it deep enough. It's not nearly as fast as the shovel, but it's the right tool for the job."

Sinclair reached down into the hole and pulled out a few handfuls of dirt. He looked up at Harry. "Looks good."

Harry shook his head. "Sinclair, I get that this is hard work, but you knew that when you signed up. I said I would teach you to do the job the right way, and I want you to learn. You can't do things halfway and expect to get the results that you want. Half the loose dirt that was in there is still there. We have to be able to see what we're doing so that we make sure this bar hits the right place. It's heavy, and I don't want to use it to do nothing, so get in there and clear the dirt out!"

Sinclair reached down and started to pull out more dirt. After a few handfuls, he looked back at Harry, who peered into the hole and shook his head. They did this a few more times until all the loose dirt was gone.

Harry stepped up to the hole and dropped the heavy bar into it. "You let the weight of the bar do the digging for you. That's why the tip is so narrow. You just have to pick it up and drop it in the right place enough times, and it will dig. Each time, it can go about three inches into the ground, but it's only maybe an inch wide. We have to break up all the loose dirt and pull it out until we're about two feet into the ground."

They went on like this for a while, with Harry dropping the post in several times and Sinclair pulling the dirt out. Sinclair started to slacken on how much he was doing before moving out of the way. Harry smiled after the third time of this happening.

"Okay, your turn!" he said just after Sinclair stood back up from clearing out a little dirt.

Harry passed him the twenty-pound metal bar and stepped back. Sinclair started out strong, but after about ten times, he was tired. Harry moved him aside and cleared out the hole the right way, and then Sinclair saw the difference. The bar could only bite into the ground a few inches, and if there was loose soil, it wouldn't go into the ground that needed to be broken up.

The work was long and hard. For the next few hours, they kept removing the dirt and small rocks, making holes. Every twenty minutes or so, they switched who was clearing out the dirt, and after Harry left the same amount in as Sinclair did a few times, the Bishop boy started to see the need to do things right.

"I get seven holes done a day, working by myself. With you, I'm hoping we can get around twelve done. The work just takes time to do it right, but as you see, the holes we have are much tighter." Harry dropped the first of the posts in. "Now we need to get the wooden maul and drive this post the rest of the way in. If we used the iron one, we would run the risk of breaking the post, which would do us no good."

Another hour passed as they put in the first of the posts. Harry kept guiding Sinclair as to how best to use a tool and where to go. As the morning wore on, Sinclair started to realize that taking his time was important.

Sinclair bushed his hands off as he looked at the post they'd put in. "I know you keep saying that it takes less effort to do things the right way the first time, but doing these holes your way seems to take a lot of work."

Harry sat down on a rock and gave a gap-toothed grin. "I'd say you're right about the amount of work it takes to do it right. I never said doing things right was easy, only that doing things right the first time took less effort."

Sinclair dropped to the ground. "Sure seems like we have put in more effort with these five than I did with the twenty yesterday."

Harry nodded slowly. "I can see where you could think that, but today, you and I have done five already. By the end of the day, we'll have done twelve. Let's say that I give you credit for six of them, and I take credit for six. That means in one day of doing them right, you did more than you did in two days before, but even if I only gave you credit for five, that's still the same number of posts."

Sinclair shook his head. "I did twenty yesterday and twenty the day before."

Harry grabbed his sides and let out a great laugh. "Boy, you did three yesterday that didn't fall over in a stiff wind. You go and push on any of the ones we put in today with all your strength, and I will go push on one of your three with just one arm. The ol' man gave you three because he knew you were hungry, but I still have to redo all the ones you did because they won't last the month."

Sinclair looked down at the ground and spoke unsteadily. "So I did it the wrong way for two days and got paid for five total, but while this way is harder, the posts will last and will not have to be redone. All my first work was essentially wasted and actually made the job harder. Doing it right the first time would have meant a lot less work."

Harry stood up and reached out his hand to help Sinclair up. "Now you have the measure of it. Do it right the first time. Let's get back to it. The work won't wait for us."

Chapter Sixteen

"If anyone alive today could explain to us how it felt to wake up to having classes one day, it would be the elves. However, they don't like talking to me."

—A primer on classes and lifebooks: Dr. Sebastian Sam, mages' school in Bukit - Two Sisters 1139

As Sinclair was working on putting in fence posts, Penelope was working at the weaving factory. She'd been trying to make sure that she did each step perfectly but couldn't figure out why she wasn't moving as quickly as everyone else. Her workspace was laid out neatly, and she had all the tools she needed. She did each step with care, slowly making sure that nothing was out of place, and fully combed the lines down after each row was added.

One of the older workers, Susan, had been watching her work for the past two days and came over to talk with her. "Penelope, you're not moving very fast with your work. Is everything okay?"

"Yes and no. I know what to do. I have all my notes, and I follow everything perfectly, but I'm just not very fast. I want to make the best that I can and be useful, but I seem too slow."

"Yes, your rows do look very neat and your area tidy." Susan sat down next to Penelope.

"I'm just worried that I'm not fast enough to make any money." Tears were starting to form in Penelope's eyes.

Susan reached over and hugged Penelope and whispered, "It's okay. We can figure this out." She smiled at the young girl. "Why don't you show me what you are doing? Maybe we can see what's making you go so slow."

For the next several minutes, Penelope worked through her steps one at a time, making sure everything was perfect after each pass. She kept her work area neat, and everything was fully in place.

Susan stopped her. "Come with me. I have someone I want you to watch. I know you watched Elle when you first got here, and it's true that she makes the best cloth we have, but I want you to watch the person who gets paid the most for her work."

Penelope looked over at Susan as she stood up. "You mean it's not Elle?"

Susan chuckled and shook her head. "No, she's not the one who makes the most. She's not even in the top ten. She makes the best cloth, but she only makes the same amount of money as the middle-of-the-road weavers."

Penelope was confused as they walked over to a group of ladies who were talking and laughing. Their work area, while organized, was not perfectly clean and tidy. Unlike Elle, they didn't seem to mind having noise around them and people talking. In fact, it almost looked like they were just spending time with their friends.

Susan said, "Ladies, I want you to meet Penelope. She learned how to do the whole process from Elle and has it down just about perfect, but... she is slow as molasses on a cold day. Can you please show what she can cut to work faster?"

"Sure!" cried one of the more cheerful-looking ladies. "Come sit by me for a bit, and I can show you what you can cut."

The next thirty minutes went on with Penelope shocked at the disregard for order and perfection. The lady only raked her lines every few passes and didn't keep everything straight. There were times when the tread rolled, and she just kept going, and some gaps showed up in the fabric. After a few minutes of moving fast, the lady slowed down, made a few adjustments, corrected the gaps that showed up by pulling everything tight, and then got to moving again. Elle would do a third as much as this lady did in the same amount of time.

Susan returned and asked, "Did you see anything that you might want to start to do on yours?"

"I am not sure," Penelope replied. "She did get more done, but the quality wasn't as good. I don't want to get my work rejected if it isn't good enough."

One lady said, "I wouldn't worry too much about that. We have several levels of fabric here, but one big rule is the amount of fabric done in a day. I can get paid for three frames in a day at the above-midgrade pay, and Elle gets one loom a day at the top pay. So I end up getting two coppers less than she does per frame, but I get three frames done."

"But shouldn't I do it the best I can, no matter what?" asked Penelope.

Susan smiled and rested her hand on Penelope's shoulder. "Yes and no. If the job doesn't get done, do you get paid? Sometimes *good enough* is what needs to happen as you learn the job and work more. You have to deliver the product to get paid."

"But should I deliver a bad product?" Penelope crinkled her nose.

"Not at all. Our factory has pay for several different levels of product that we create. We have uses for roughly made fabric and for the smoothest we can weave. So even if you mess the whole thing up, as long as you finish a loom, you'll get paid something. You should try to do a good job, but here, delivering a product is the most important thing, not being perfect. Kind of like at home—an okay breakfast that you eat is better than a perfect one you can't eat because you have to be somewhere."

***

Warren saw his siblings coming back to the wagon at the end of their day of work. He was hiding at the edge of the forest, where they couldn't see him. He didn't want to face them because he didn't have anything to show for all the trapping that he'd done. At the end of the day, he'd managed to find a bush that had berries but didn't have a container to bring them back with him, so he'd just eaten his fill.

As Warren came out of the woods and approached the wagon, he saw Gretchen. He noticed that she quickly hid a small paper bag of candy in the right pocket of her skirt. She waved to him and opened the door, and they walked in. Sinclair and Penelope were already inside.

Sinclair caught his eye. "Now that Warren has gotten back, I guess we can have dinner. What did everyone bring?"

Penelope put three loaves of bread on the old table, along with four pears and part of a wheel of cheese. "I ended up doing much better today, so I was able to get enough for dinner tonight," she said proudly. "The women there showed me that I was trying to be too perfect and so was unable to get enough done. Once they showed me that *good and delivered* was better than *perfect and undelivered*, I was able to make some adjustments."

Sinclair smirked. "Dad used to tell me, 'Perfect is the enemy of good.' I think that's kind of what they showed you."

"Yes, that seems to fit," Penelope said as she cut the bread. "I never understood why Mom would get frustrated with me when I would take everything off the shelf when I was putting new products out. I kind of understand now. Jobs have to get done, but they don't always have to be perfect. It was nice getting paid today."

"Today went great for me!" Gretchen took a bite of a pear. "I went back to the Higginses, but *th*ey didn't need me today. So Mrs. Higgins sent me over to *th*e candy store, and I helped Mrs. Cadbury work on her books. I wish I could have helped make *th*e candy, but *th*ey said that takes a lot of skill, and unless I take *th*at as a class, I wouldn't be making candy as good or as fast as *th*ey could."

"How much did you get paid?" Penelope asked hopefully.

"Well... umm... see, I got lunch. And it was nice, and I told *th*em that I'd been paid in product yesterday, so *th*ey paid me in candy today. So I have a piece for each of you." She smiled and pulled a bag out of her left pocket.

Warren sent Gretchen a confused look as he looked at her other pocket. She gave him a quick nod, confirming his suspicions, and he nodded a little as he took his piece of peppermint from the bag she had produced, knowing she would give him more later.

"Gretch! We need money so that we can have real food, not hats and candy," Penelope said.

Sinclair cleared his throat and gave Penelope a stern look. "We have dinner, and a little treat is nice, but I do think her math is worth more than four pieces of candy. Gretchen, you need to do better on getting your value when you work."

"I know. I'm just no good at negotiating. I want *th*e work so much that I don't want to run *th*e risk of *th*em turning me away..." She finished up her bread. "So, Sinclair, how did your day go?"

"Well, much better! I got invited back tomorrow to keep working, which is great, and I got paid for half of the holes, which was much better than yesterday. I learned how to use a digging bar and how to split rails with wedges and a hammer. It was a fun day but lots of hard work. It was nice that my posts actually stayed standing and I didn't have to repeat my work like before." Sinclair sat back in his chair. He pulled out twenty copper coins and set them on the table. "So, tomorrow is our last day in this town. The timer shows twenty-four hours."

Sinclair took a big breath then let it out.

"I'm going to go to the farm and get back here with four hours left so that we can get everything together that we need. I'll pick my class when I get back from working. I'm still not sure if I want that trader class or the store clerk one. Either way, we need to be ready to leave when the timer is low."

He took another pause, looking at Penelope. "Pen, you and Gretch need to spend tomorrow finding out what you can about our next town, Deal, and what we can buy low here and sell high there. Just like Dad taught us."

Chapter Seventeen

"Sometimes, your best friend is dumb, but that's okay."

—Rikwast, chief foreman, second division, Royal Engineers for King Edward V - Before Two Sisters 150

"When your friend calls you dumb, you first need to ask if they are dumb. If they aren't, then what they say might be true, or they could just be messing with you again."

—Gabrid Flintback, chief foreman, first division, Royal Engineers for King Edward V -Before Two Sisters 150

The next morning, after they washed up, Sinclair did what his dad always did and set the agenda for the day so everyone would know what was expected.

"So, today, we're going to make sure we're ready to go," Sinclair said as they were finishing up their breakfast of day-old bread and nuts. "I'm going to work on the farm for one more day to make us some more money. Pen, you and Gretch go ask around about our next town, which is Deal. See what you can find out about it and what they might want."

"We don't have much money, so we'll wait till you get back before we buy anything." Penelope pulled out a list. "That way, we have the most that we can get. We'll also wait for you to come and try to haggle since you're better at that than I am. The ladies at the factory mentioned few merchants that might know about other towns, so we're going to stop in there and talk with them. There's also the dispatch office we passed on the way to the factory, which might give some additional information. I tried to find the town in Grandpa's journals, but we have so many of them, and it's hard to find anything about a town named Deal when he talks about making deals so much as well."

"I'm going to stop in and see if *th*e hatter's wife or *th*e candy maker knows any*th*ing about Deal and what *th*ey might want or need," Gretchen said.

Penelope scribbled something down on her list and looked over at Gretchen. "Great idea. I've added them to the list of places to go. We only have the first half of the day to find out what we want to take with us, and then we have to leave the last few hours for Slair to buy it for us."

"Pen, what do you have for me to help with today?" Warren moved over to look at Penelope's list on the table.

"Umm, well, sweeping out the wagon and preparing to leave would be good. It has gotten a little dirty in here, and we'll need space to carry the goods we're buying. I'm sure Honor will want your company."

Sinclair grabbed his hat and jumped out of the wagon. "I'll see you guys tonight!" he called as he headed off toward the farm for the last time. As he walked south, away from the town, the two girls went to line up at the gate.

"So, where do you want to start first?" Gretchen asked.

Penelope checked her list. "Well, I was wanting to ask the general store if they did any trading with Deal. You can go talk to the hatter and candy maker's wives to see what they might know. After that, we should meet at the dispatch office to find out if they can tell us anything. They might be doing mail runs that way."

"Sounds good to me," Gretchen said softly as she smiled and bounced on her feet.

The two girls made their way into town. As they neared the town center, they hugged and parted ways. Gretchen made her way to the hat shop as she ran her hands over the bonnet she was wearing. She smiled, thinking of all the things in the shop. Surely, taking hats to the next town would be what they needed to do. Pretty little things, like bonnets and ribbons, had to be the best things in the world, she thought. Until she thought of candy, and then she knew that it had to be candy that she and her siblings should take. Bags and bags of candy. She would have to sneak a few bits as well.

She smiled as she walked into the hattery. "Hi, Mr. Higgins. Is Mrs. Higgins around?"

"Yes, lil' miss. I'll let her know you're here. Is there anything I can tell her?"

"I just want to see what all she knows about Deal."

"Oh my. Deal is a fine little town. The issue is getting there. The brigands have gotten to be quite the problem, and we've almost lost contact going that way. Hold on a moment, and I'll grab my wife." Mr. Higgins walked through the door behind the counter. A few minutes later, Gretchen was sitting with Mrs. Higgins at their kitchen table, talking.

"Well, Deal is a mining town, so they're all about the mine," Mrs. Higgins said. "There's little else up there, though they have a great view. They're only about sixty miles away, and Collina used to do lots of trading with them. Then, about a year ago, the robbing started, and now we don't do much trade. There's still a once-a-month wagon that comes down from there under heavy guard, but that's it."

"What types of *th*ings did *th*ey use to trade for *th*e most?" Gretchen asked.

"Well, food was a big thing. They don't have much room for growing on the side of the mountain, and most of the people up there are involved in the mine. Honestly, I would think they would want anything and everything with how limited they are right now. We never sent anything up there since it was just too far away and too few people needed nice hats."

"Do you know anyone else I should ask?"

"The innkeeper and the general store might know more since the wagon drivers talk with both of them. What made you want to ask about Deal, anyway?"

"Well, we *th*ink *th*at's our next stop on our way home. I wanted to know if *th*ere was something we could buy here and sell *th*ere. That type of *th*ing," Gretchen said.

After visiting the hat shop, Gretchen made her way over to the candy store, where she found much the same information that Mrs. Higgins had given her. While the suggestion that they take hard candy came up, as everyone liked candy and not everywhere had a candy store, Gretchen told Mrs. Cadbury that she needed to talk with her siblings about that. She left with another piece of hard candy.

Chapter Eighteen

"Dungeons have different ranks given to them by the Adventurer's Guild. Those range from one to ten, based on how hard they are to beat. As the number goes up, so does the danger, but the rewards get bigger and better as well. The one in our town has a rank of three, so it's an easy one for most to make it through, and the rewards are okay but not great."

—Charles Bishop, teaching his kids

The girls met back up and shared what they'd found before heading over to the dispatch office. While Gretchen was visiting with the two ladies and asking questions, Penelope had gone to the inn, tailor, blacksmith, grocer, baker, and general store about what was best to buy and who to buy it from. All they had left was the dispatcher.

"I'm not sure what else we're going to learn at the dispatch office, but we want to make sure we know as much as we can before we make any buys. Dad always told us that when you're making a deal, knowledge is key," Penelope said as they made their way to their last stop.

"But I *th*ought he said relationships are the most important *th*ing when making a deal," Gretchen said as she struggled to keep up.

"Well, yes, I guess he said both more than once. But knowledge is what we need right now, not relationships. Without knowledge, we won't know what to buy, and we don't have time to make relationships to get the knowledge we need." Penelope pulled open the door to the dispatch.

In front of them stood a tall wooden counter and a scale. Behind the counter was a spool of twine and a stack of papers, and in the middle sat a little bell and hammer. Penelope walked right up and hit the bell twice with the hammer. *Ding ding.*

"Be right with you!" an old-sounding man yelled from the back.

Penelope pulled out her list and read it over. She'd written key words and phrases that people had said to her next to each name. Then she crossed her arms and looked expectantly at the back of the building, huffing and sighing. After a few moments, an old man with a cane came out of the back.

"Yes, young ladies. How can I help you two today?" he asked with a warm smile.

Penelope pulled out her list. "Well, we have a few questions that we were hoping you could answer for us. You see, we're getting ready to head over to Deal and would like to know what types of trade goods they're deficient in."

The clerk pulled on his short beard with his free hand. "Well... not sure that I do. I'm not in the trading business, so that isn't something that I would do much of."

"Hm… besides the inn, tailor, candy shop, blacksmith, hatter, grocer, baker, and general store, do you know anyone we could talk to who might know the answer?"

"Nope, can't say that I do, young lady. Now, if you will excuse me, I have work to do—unless, of course, you're wanting to send a dispatch."

"No, that's everything." Penelope turned and headed out the door.

Gretchen looked up at the old man and pulled out the bag of candy Mrs. Cadbury had given her. "Would you like a *c*andy, mister?" she asked in her quiet voice.

The clerk smiled down at her. "Thank you, little one. It has been a while since I had any." He pulled a butterscotch from the bag and popped it into his mouth.

"Mrs. Cadbury and Mrs. Higgins both told me *th*at if anyone knew what Deal was always needing, it would be you, since you handle *th*e writing for all *th*e dispatches. We're heading home, and it looks like *th*at's our next stop on *th*e way *th*ere, so we wanted to buy some*th*ing here *th*at we could take *th*ere and sell. That's why we came in here."

Gretchen sighed and looked out the window at her older sister. Then she turned and to the old man again. "Penelope means well, but she's always worrying about her lists and trying to get *th*ings done fast, so she comes off as rude sometimes. I'm sorry for the way that she acted. Please don't be mad at her."

The old clerk chuckled. "Well, she was kind of straightforward with her questions. Caught me off guard. I was expecting a customer, not you two, so I didn't respond as nicely as I could have." He grabbed a piece of paper and a quill. "I'll make you a list of things they used to get from us. They haven't done much trading in the past year because of the bandits. So you be careful, and you might want to see if a guard will go with you. Unless your dad is a big one." He started making his list. When he was done, he passed the paper to her. "Here you go, miss. Be safe as you go, and thanks for the candy and the smile."

Gretchen waved and smiled at him. As she left the store, she said over her shoulder, "Thank you so much!"

As Gretchen came out of the dispatch office, Penelope walked over to her in a huff. "What took you so long? We have things we have to do, and the man in there didn't know anything at all. Just like most of the other people I talked to today. No one knows what they want since they're not trading with Deal right now!"

"Pen, the nice old man in *th*ere gave me a list of the *th*ings Deal might want in trade, based on what they used to want and what *th*e dispatches he wrote or read told him," Gretchen said with a smile as she handed the paper to her list-loving sister.

"What? But he said he didn't know anything!" Penelope stomped her foot.

A few minutes, later the girls were deep in talk about what was best to buy to take with them. It was hard to decide. They had some room on the wagon, but one whole section was nothing but shelves they couldn't get through, and the girls knew quality goods when they saw them from working with their parents, but the prices were all different.

They spent the rest of the afternoon looking for items on the dispatcher's list they that they could buy cheaply and mark up to sell to the mining town. Their best idea was to buy rolls of fabric since Collina made cloth in their factory and Deal didn't. The girls could buy the end rolls for cheap and sell them to the tailor in Deal. They would spend any leftover money to buy hard candy because everyone liked that. Gretchen didn't tell Penelope that she already had a small bag in her pocket. She wanted more.

With that, the girls walked happily back to the wagon, not talking much. They planned to meet Warren there and wait for Sinclair to get back. The last four hours would be busy. They had a plan, which made Penelope happy, and Gretchen had her candy, which made her happy. But their mood quickly changed to dismay when they got back to the wagon and found Warren wasn't there.

Chapter Nineteen

"Many think that classes give people power in their skills and abilities that can't be matched without those classes. That's not true. I have seen a housewife with no merchant class out-haggle a level-twenty store clerk."

—*Grandpa Bishop*

Where's Warren? He should be here by now!" Gretchen said.

"I bet he ran off into the woods again. He's always playing around when there are things to do," Sinclair said.

"We only have three hours left before the wagon moves, and we haven't gone to buy any of the fabric," Pen said to her brother. "If Warren doesn't get here soon, we're going to have to get as much stuff as we can out of the wagon so that we have something to sell here when our ride leaves us."

"Let's give him another hour, and then we can start to pack," Sinclair said. "I'm still hoping he gets back soon so we can go buy the fabric, but if he doesn't, we can't spend the money on that since we won't have any place to sleep."

Gretchen looked up from her chair. "Maybe I should go look for him to see if I can get him to come back faster."

Sinclair shook his head and sighed. "No. If you go look for him and he comes back, then you'll be out there, not knowing when to come back and not here to help us unload. There's no use. We just have to wait and hope he gets here soon."

"We're not leaving him here, so we need to start getting ready to unload if we have to," Pen said.

They started to pull together what meager things they had that were useful without the wagon. They bundled their dishes into bags and moved

all the food they'd managed not to eat into a basket. They didn't have much, so the work was quick.

"If we had a backup plan of where to go, then we would know if pulling out the furniture made sense or not," Sinclair said as the last of their bags were packed.

"What are we going to do with Honor?" asked Gretchen, looking at the cat, who was sound asleep on her window ledge.

"I guess right before the wagon leaves, we grab her and pull her out," Penelope replied. "She pretty much takes care of herself with the hunting she does, so not much will change there. She'll just be without her window."

Sinclair shook his head and furrowed his brow. "I'm not happy that

we have to leave Grandpa's books and the maps in the wagon, but since we don't know where we're sleeping, they'll just weigh us down and get ruined when it rains."

When the timer was down to thirty minutes, they started to unload the wagon. Warren was not back yet, so the siblings had decided it was better to stay together even if it meant losing the wagon. However, Sinclair was frustrated. "Dad told me once that people sacrifice themselves for those they love, and there are times when we have to do things that make us sad or angry, but if it means keeping the people we love safe, it's something that just needs to happen."

"Grandpa's journal said that every action has a cost," Sinclair said to the girls as they were looking at their things on the ground. "He called it 'opportunity cost.' If we leave without Warren, then we lose all the opportunities of everything that we could do with him. If we stay, we lose the opportunities of the things that we could do with the wagon, like get home."

As the timer moved down to ten minutes, Gretchen, who was holding Honor and crying, saw a small kid with a pack running their way, waving to them.

"Look, it's Warren. He made it!" yelled Gretchen as she tossed the big cat back into the wagon.

Honor meowed and walked in a circle till she was looking back out the door. She sat tall, like a royal looking over her subjects, raising her nose and watching. They had less than ten minutes. The older children threw their things back into the wagon and yelled to their brother to hurry up. It was quite a sight as the things that had been piled on the ground were unceremoniously shoved back in. It was good that they hadn't taken much more out of the wagon, as there was no way they would have had the time to recover all the items.

After the children climbed into the wagon, Sinclair slid the door closed and held it shut with his back. He pulled on his hair as he screamed at Warren. "We almost missed the move because of you! We had no idea where you were, so we were going to miss going home so that we wouldn't leave you! What were you thinking?"

Warren held up two sets of rabbits. "You always said I was too little and that I should just do nothing all day, but I wanted to help. All you wanted me to do was clean up the wagon and keep the cat! I wanted to show that I could bring home food too! So that's what I did all day. While you were working someplace, digging holes, I was getting us food! See? I have these, and I have a bag full of nuts and berries and even those wild onions you like!"

Penelope grabbed Warren in a big hug and whispered, "We thought that we'd lost you and were going to have to find you. We thought we weren't going to get home. We had no idea where you were. I'm so sorry. You are capable, and I should have treated you that way."

Gretchen smiled and hugged Warren too. There were tear marks on her face where she'd been crying. Penelope had them too.

Right as Warren started to speak, the wagon shook. It was moving once again.

CHAPTER TWENTY

"Cats? Don't like them. Why do you ask?"

—Dr. Sebastian Sam, mages' school in Bukit - Two Sisters 1139

The children rushed out of the wagon and looked around. Whereas Collina was in pastureland consisting of rolling hills and small fields, Deal was nestled in the side of a mountain, which wrapped around the town on three sides. Several small streams ran through it. Where Collina had a palisade, Deal had an eight-foot-high stone wall running from one edge of the mountain to the other. There were several wooden platforms and watchtowers down the edge of the wall and a large wooden gate. Outside the wall were a few small fields and the Bishops' very large, very conspicuous wagon.

Sinclair opened his lifebook. "It looks like we're here just for eighteen hours. We won't have much time to figure out what we need to take with us for the next town, and we don't have anything to sell."

The children looked back and forth at each other for a moment. Then the gates opened, and a group of five guards came toward them. As the guards got close, four of them stopped, and the fifth walked a few more steps. This guard had a half cape and held his helmet under his arm.

"Honored guests, may I ask your intentions here?" he asked.

Sinclair stepped forward. "We're here to see about buying goods and then traveling on. We don't want to be much of a bother to you and should be gone by this time tomorrow."

"Are you a merchant, then, or wanderers? We don't take kindly to thieves, as we have had to deal with too many of them of late, and our gates are already closed for the night," the guard said gruffly.

"I'm a merchant. Well, soon I will be, and this is my family," Sinclair said, motioning to the other kids.

"So you're not classed as of yet?" the guard asked.

"No, I was about to pick it," Sinclair replied.

"All unclassed in town must consult with the town council and select the class they deem best. Please come with us now to see them." The guard started to turn.

At that moment, Honor hopped out of the wagon door. She approached the guard and walked between his legs and then around everyone else, meowing a bit angrily. She then sat down between the guards and the children and stared at him. Her tail twitched back and forth, and she let out a long, low meow that sounded like she was issuing a decree.

The guard moved back a half step, looking like he'd seen a ghost. He spoke in a shaking voice. "Oh my—you again. I'm sorry. I didn't mean any harm." He turned to Sinclair. "Please have your class selected before coming into town tomorrow. I'm sure we'll welcome renewed trade with the Wonderful Wandering Wagon. It has been a long time, and most of the town is too young to remember you."

He then bowed to Honor and returned to the other four guards. They headed back toward town. After they passed through the gate, it closed with a thunk.

The Bishops looked at Honor in confusion as the purring cat sauntered back to the wagon. She jumped up and looked over her shoulder. She chirped at them once before walking out of their line of sight.

Penelope was the first to snap out of it. "Slair, I think we need to get back in the wagon and have you pick your class, or we might end up with you as a miner or something."

"Yeah, *th*at sounds like a good idea," Gretchen chimed in.

Sinclair nodded and started back toward the wagon, dazed from the events that had just transpired. As he entered it, he was focused on trying to figure out what the guard meant by "trade with the Wonderful Wandering Wagon" and also why he'd seemed so put off by Honor.

Warren rushed past Sinclair and jumped into the wagon ahead of him. Once they were all inside, they found Honor on her pillow. She was trying to look asleep, but her tail gave her away. It was twitching back and forth like she was keyed up and ready to pounce on a mouse. Warren rushed over, wrapped his arms around the huge fluffy cat, and buried his face in her fur.

"Honor, you're great. I don't know what you did, but you did something and saved us—I'm sure of it. Thank you, Honor! You're the best cat in the whole world!" he exclaimed as he picked her up and dropped to the floor, petting her.

Honor, for her part, tolerated the child and even started purring loudly as she was scratched under her chin. It was clear that she thought she was worthy of the praise of being the best cat in the world.

Gretchen was the last in the wagon, and she closed the door and dropped the latch. There was little light coming through the window, so she set a slow match to burn and lit their two candles. She sat down on her bed, which was the second from the bottom.

"So, I guess I need to pick my class," Sinclair said.

Penelope pulled out her page of notes. "If my notes are right, then you have access to the following classes: Farmhand, Store Clerk, Beggar, and Tolerable Trekking Trader. That last one sounds the most interesting. I'm guessing you have access to farmhand because of the work you were doing, store clerk because of Dad's store, beggar because we've had to ask for lots of food, and the last one because of the wagon. Is there anything else you can tell us about the choices?"

Sinclair sat up in his chair and called up his lifebook. "Hold on—I want to check them out again to see if anything has changed." As he was speaking, Honor jumped into his lap and curled up, taking up all the room. "Looks like the options have changed for me. I now have Miner and Tolerable Trekking Trader, and it looks like I have Royal Groomer. That is an odd one," he muttered. "Let me flip to see what it does."

Just then, Honor hopped off his lap and back up to her perch, where she sat tall, looking at Sinclair.

"Well, that's odd. The Royal Groomer was a purple option, which meant it was an ultra-rare class, but it's gone now. In fact, the only option I now have is the Tolerable Trekking Trader. It's flashing, and I can't even close my lifebook," Sinclair said in frustration.

"I guess you have one choice. Might as well take it," Gretchen said softly.

"Yeah... I have never heard of a class selection that would not let you close your book. I'm going to have to take it," Sinclair said.

As Sinclair selected the class, the empty oil lamp in the ceiling of the wagon emitted a light like a large lightstone. The old worn-out bunks and chairs morphed, becoming sleek and well finished. The boards the children had been sleeping on became down-stuffed mattresses covered by light blankets, green with red edges, matching the color of the wagon. The curtains went from threadbare cloth to lovely yellow lace with embroidered red cat paws on the bottom. Lastly, the rusted potbelly stove turned all black and smooth like it was a well-used and well-loved item.

***

All the children yelped in amazement as they looked around. Gretchen seemed most astonished, as she'd been sitting on wood that changed to a mattress. Honor jumped from her pillow to the bookshelf. She walked across the top of the books until she got to one that had not been there before. With her paw, she pushed a little, and it slid out just a hair. None of the children were looking at her. She did it again, and still, no one was paying her mind. She even meowed, but they were too busy talking among themselves to even hear her or pay her any mind. Having no other options, she did what she always loathed doing, which was to push books over. Sure, a cup or a candle was fun to knock over—even more fun if she could slide something off onto someone's head—but books just shouldn't be mistreated.

Thud! The small but heavy book hit the wooden floor, snapping the children out of their excitement at seeing the wagon change in the front of them. Warren, who was the closest to the fallen book, picked it up and stared at it. On the front was a beautifully painted picture of the wagon. Across the top of the book was embossed in gold leaf, *The Wonderful Wandering Wagon*. He tried to open it but was unable.

Warren turned to Sinclair. "I think that this is for you. It might be about how your class works."

Sinclair took the book, and it opened with a flash of light. It drew his lifebook out of his hand, and they both floated upward. The two books met in the air a foot from Sinclair's nose, where the new book lay open on top of the lifebook and sank into it.

The Bishops looked at each other with awe as the lifebook fell back into Sinclair's open hand. No one said or did anything until Honor bumped her head onto the hand holding the book. Sinclair looked down as the book's pages started to turn. His eyes twitched back and forth. He was reading quickly, moving through dozens of pages that were flipping on their own. His mouth opened in amazement.

"Guys, this wagon is more than just a way to get around. It's part of my class. I wish I'd taken it when I first got the option to take a class because then things would have been so much simpler. As a Tolerable Trekking Trader, I'm given five gold pieces to start my business with, and it says I'm contracted with the owner of the

Wonderful Wandering Wagon. Every quarter, they are to be paid 22.17 percent of what it calls 'net income.' Yearly, I am to give a written report about the use of the funds and the reason for any wagon adjustments and expansions. After three years, I'm able to renegotiate my contract and leave employment. It also says that anyone who travels in the WWW is subject to a nonnegotiable nondisclosure agreement regarding the nature of the business arrangement with the partner and the abilities of the wagon itself. There's even a page that shows the previous partners of the wagon. Dad ran the wagon before he met Mom, and Grandpa too. No wonder Mom was being so weird."

"What does that mean?" Ren asked, picking up Honor again.

"That means our parents know exactly where we are, and we somehow have five gold pieces to buy supplies for our store," Penelope replied. "They've been preparing us all along. We just have to keep good books along the way."

"Guess *th*at means first *th*ing in the morning, we have to see what's for sale and what the next town on the trip needs," Gretchen said. "We did this before, but with five gold pieces, we have a real budget, so we can buy things and move." She yawned and climbed back into bed. "Slair, see if you can find a way to turn off the light in here. I'm tired."

EPILOGUE

"Well, I guess Honor was listening to us talk," Grandpa Bishop said to the other three. "Not quite what I meant when I was saying I wanted to send Sinclair with a library, but taking all my journals might help. There are some good books on how to run a store and, if things haven't changed too much, some details on what to expect."

"That was not what I meant when I said that I didn't think Sinclair was ready to be alone, but I guess I did this to myself," Mary Bishop stated, smoothing the blanket on her lap. "Still, I'm not happy with Honor for taking all the kids on this trip. I know your family contracted out to her dad, but honestly, aren't the others a little young to be out there by themselves?"

"Well, dear, they aren't by themselves. They have each other. The wagon and Honor will help guide them. After all, she gets a cut in the profits as well. She won't let them starve. Besides, I know that I would have loved to have someone with me on my route. It should keep them grounded, and they'll learn to depend on each other." Charles Bishop reached over to hold his wife's hand.

"Since they all found the wagon, I fully expect that with the four of them there, they managed to get Sinclair his trader class and started selling even in the first town they hit," Charles continued. "It should be Collina, which was such a fun town in my day. They had the best textiles in the area. If the kids played their cards right, they would have used the seed money that came with Sinclair's class to buy a load and sell at the next town, which should be Deal. I'm sure they're fine. Our kids are smart."

Grandma Bishop crinkled her nose and sipped her tea. "I guess we should expect them back in a couple of years, if I recall how long a circuit is. I guess it will be quiet for a while."

The four adults lapsed into silence as they watched the fire, drinking their tea, each caught up in thoughts about what was to come. The men, who had been out with Honor before, were relaxed, and the only one who seemed truly worried about the situation was Mary Bishop.

"Do you think we could go see them at one of the stops?" Mary asked her husband.

THE ADVENTURE IS JUST BEGINNING...

go to www.wonderfulwanderingwagon.com for the latest updates about the series and to see what new books, coloring sheets, workbooks and lesson plans we've released.

Thank You

TO OUR EARLY SUPPORTERS AND KICKSTARTER BACKERS!

WE COULDN'T HAVE DONE IT WITHOUT YOU!

Bill and Freda Roberson
Ron and Irene Lambright
Teresa Stone
Richard Miller
John and Leslie Wilson
Andrea and Charlie Moss
Chris Heivly
Joshua C. Chadd
Shari Roberson
Robert & Michelle Harger
Matthew Barron

Thank You

to the author community who has been so kind and welcoming to us!

to Andrew Peterson for sharing the totatoes and charrots with us
for more information check out The Wingfeather Saga
https://www.wingfeathersaga.com/

The Rabbit Room Community
www.rabbitroom.com

The Realm Makers Community
www.realmmakers.com

Jonathan Rogers and the Habit Community
https://thehabit.co/

to Shay and Kenneth at Wolfbane Books for the great publishing advice
www.wolfbanebooks.com

Moody Publishers
www.moodypublishers.com

Connor Boyak and the Tuttle Twins team
www.tuttletwins.com and www.tuttletwinstv.com

S.D. Smith
www.sdsmith.com

The Harmon Brothers Team for all the help with our sales pages and launch video.

The Tech Beans Community in Columbia, SC.

The One Million Cups Columbia Chapter

www.ingramcontent.com/pod-product-compliance
Lightning Source LLC
LaVergne TN
LVHW100316210926
848480LV00003B/1147

* 9 7 8 1 9 5 9 1 5 8 0 1 1 *